HEALTHY CHURCHES

GOD'S BIBLE BLUEPRINT FOR GROWTH

BRIAN JOHNSTON

Healthy Churches: God's Bible Blueprint For Growth

Copyright © 2015 by Brian Johnston

Book and Cover design by Hayden Press. For information contact : haydenpress2011@gmail.com

If you enjoy reading this book, please consider taking a moment to leave a positive review on Amazon.

ISBN: 978-1508726098

First Edition: March 2015

10 9 8 7 6 5 4 3 2 1

CONTENTS

1: FACING THE CHALLENGES

Clovis Chappell, a minister from over a century ago, used to tell the story of two paddleboats in the USA. They left Memphis about the same time, and were both travelling down the Mississippi River to New Orleans. As they sailed side by side, sailors on one boat made a few remarks about what they saw as the slow progress of the other boat. Soon challenges were made, and a race began. Competition became fierce as the two boats roared through the Deep South. One boat began falling behind as it ran out of fuel. There had been plenty of coal for the trip, but not enough for a race. As the boat dropped back, an enterprising sailor took some of the ship's cargo and started using it as fuel. When the sailors saw that the supplies burned almost as well as the coal, they fuelled their boat with the material they'd been given to transport from Memphis to New Orleans. They ended up winning the race, but burning their cargo.

God has entrusted cargo to us, too. By 'cargo' I mean Bible truth, if you'll permit me to refer to it in that way (compare 1 Timothy 6:20). Our job is to do our part in seeing that this cargo reaches its destination. We hear a lot today about programs to help churches grow faster. But when the church program takes priority over truth, the testimony of the Lord suffers. If the fastest growing churches have dispensed with even some of the cargo of truth which God has given us, then who would dare call that success? What 'go faster' strategies can we see in operation today? There's the 'Big is beautiful' way of thinking. 25% of churchgoers in the United Kingdom are said to be part of a congregation that's over 400-strong. Now, a whole lot of things could motivate that trend: perhaps it's a retreat into the comfort zone of a religious ghetto; or it could be a desire for anonymity or a means of avoiding having to take personal responsibility. After a busy week at work, it might be tempting just to want to 'chill out' at church. Perhaps, the desire to be associated with something big is driven by a wrong view of success. The God of the Bible is a God who specializes in minorities and who works through remnants. The Bible's measure of authenticity is not numerical. The 'megachurch' phenomenon was not there at the beginning of Christianity. The number of disciples in Jerusalem did quickly grow into thousands, but the internal evidence of the Bible is that they met in smaller units or companies all belonging to the one Church of God at Jerusalem (see Acts 4:23 Revised Version).

Which brings us back to the original mould or pattern of Christianity...but is it realistic to keep all the cargo of truth intact and still experience church growth at this time in the western world? What are some of the major challenges which face us? In Christian circles, as in any area of life, the 'grass-is-greener somewhere else' syndrome exists. It breeds discontent in the local church. People leave to go to another place of worship in a search, they say, for one which has more on offer for their children, or a more appealing 'worship' style – perhaps one designed to be attractive to outsiders to Christianity.

When we measure this against the Bible, don't we begin to see this trend exposed as not being the solution to Christianity's growth problem? Nowhere in the New Testament is any encouragement given to the idea that it's okay for Christians to transfer their allegiance based on what seems to meet their needs best at any given stage of their lives. Doesn't that inevitably betray a lack of deep conviction about the shape of Christian service and discipleship as it's prescribed for us in God's Word? Actions like that simply reflect our consumer society, one in which 'I', 'me' and 'my' seem to dominate, and where human choices get superimposed upon the divine choice for how Christians are to serve God.

Sometimes people 'move on' just because they're bored. It's a serious thing if any of us contribute to making Christianity seem boring to others. A sense of tiredness with what has seemingly become routine, can slowly turn into contempt for it. This is a problem, for if we've become bored with it, how will we be able to present it attractively to others? Then there's the fact that work can dominate the lives of those who are in employment. For those in career structures, work can easily begin to take over our lives. It's a fact that males in employment are tempted to save their best for work: and that's understandable because there's a lot of pressure coming from society to say our true sense of significance lies there. And there's that old expression, the 'Generation gap' – but perhaps with a new twist these days. Today the tie with older generations is often broken due to the very different opportunities for youth which are to be found in new technologies outside of traditional career patterns. As a result, older generations tend not to understand or feel connected with younger generations. Instead of being able to pass on the experience and wisdom of the years to those of the next generation, they tend to feel it's all foreign to them – and perhaps even feel that a patronising sneer has replaced a time-honoured respect. This is just something in the background which contributes to the fracturing of society, and to the view that only new ideas are relevant – and that certainly doesn't help Biblical Christianity.

Next, we come to consider lifestyle pressures – and there are quite a few issues in this category. Changes throughout society in the use of Sunday pose a challenge to church attendance. A day that was formerly reserved for at least nominally religious purposes, or just plain rest, has now been usurped by overtime at work, prime-time for shopping, not to mention full programmes of professional sports and other public events which draw vast crowds of people. Besides all that, so many families are broken, that it's often the time when the children who live with one parent during weekdays transfer to have their access to the other parent at weekends.

Modern media give easy, private access to such devastatingly detrimental things as pornography. In past generations the same temptations were there but they weren't so obvious. It's been illustrated like this: it's as if a past generation walked down a corridor and on the doors leading off the corridor were names like pornography; but the doors were closed – maybe not locked – but at least they were closed. Now, and for some time, rising generations in walking down that same corridor find the same doors with the same names, but the huge difference is: all the doors are wide open. Access is so much easier, and the illusion of gratification and fulfilment is made to look very inviting. Many become compulsively addicted, after beginning to look for true satisfaction where it can't be found.

There's also the fact that the media is hostile to Christianity – and, of course, it has the microphone. What I mean by that is that the message that's being constantly reinforced is an anti-Christian agenda, and it's hard for Christians to get their voice heard in a fair and unedited way. The reality is that the intellectual case for atheism is weaker than the intellectual case for Christianity, but you'd never guess it from the media's reporting. Child abuse scandals especially in institutionalised religions have, of course, helped this negative portrayal. Often Christians in the media are stereotyped in a negative way; in any panel the religious spokesperson will be the one assumed to be biased. The distinctively Christian voice has become marginalised. A society which is increasingly secular is one which has largely driven religion from public life, and forced it into the realm of the private. Thinking about it, the environment for Christianity in the western world is coming more and more to resemble its original hostile environment in the days of the pagan Roman Empire. Christians then were treated with suspicion, made scapegoats, and victims of smear campaigns.

Until now, we've been thinking about external pressures, but there are also internal difficulties which are often associated with emotionally draining relationships, conflict and disputes. At best these are a distraction, at worst they sap the desire to grow. Psychological or personality disorders and power plays are particularly debilitating. Sadly, the evidence shows that true believers in whom these disorders have long been ingrained – perhaps from early childhood experiences - can be self-deluded to the point of being impervious to counsel. Their self-promoting strategies and compulsive behaviours and win-at-all-costs attitude, which are feared in a secular business management setting, can make a church an unattractive place to be for others, mainly because all endeavours to work as a team become fraught with tension. When a church cannot evidence genuine enjoyment from being in each other's company; when it can't model an attractive, authentic Christian community spirit; then it's in deep trouble. Jesus emphasized to his disciples, before he left them, that the best advert for Christianity was that the world should be able to look on and see their evident love for one another (John 13:35).

The road to spiritual maturity is through emotional maturity. This is implied by Paul's early commentary on the Church of God at Corinth. For he says he couldn't speak to them as you would speak to spiritually-minded people for the reason that there was divisiveness and in-fighting among them, complete with strife, envying and jealousies (1 Corinthians 3:1-3). In other words, they weren't even emotionally mature. When this is the case there's a strong possibility churches will shrink rather than grow.

2: UNDERSTANDING THE TIMES

It has been widely recognised that the toughest environment for the growth of Christianity right now is in the western world, and nowhere more so than Western Europe. Church growth figures there are significantly lower than in countries where Christians are being persecuted. The question may then be asked: 'Can western churches grow today as their counterparts do in the East or in developing countries?' There, in certain places at least, the ground is more fertile, more receptive, for the spread of Biblical Christianity. Allow me to put the contrast into some kind of perspective by contrasting national attitudes to prayer between West and East in today's world. Towards the end of the last decade, in the United Kingdom, a nurse was suspended for simply offering prayer to a patient. She was subsequently reinstated, but the episode showed the unacceptability, as judged by society, of a professional person offering prayer while engaged in performing her professional duties.

By contrast, I was standing at the check-in of one international airport in the Far East. My usual flight pattern had been changed, and I'd been too distracted to notice, so the end result was that I turned up at the airport a day early for my flight! Politely, the young lady informed me that I was not due to fly until the next day. "Is there any possibility of getting a flight today?" I asked. She checked the availability on the computer, and told me that while there was space on the second flight, sadly, there was none on the first flight – and I needed both, of course, as they were connecting flights. Without a moment's hesitation, she then suggested that I go away, find a seat, and pray about the matter! Of course, I was more than happy to do this. Five minutes later the public address system crackled into life, calling my name, and asking me to return to the check-in, where she greeted me with a smile: problem solved, a seat had now become available. I noted it was 26K – I had even been allocated a window seat, always my preference!

That's all that's relevant to the point that we're making about contrasting attitudes to prayer in society between West and East - but you may be interested to know there was a sequel to the story thus far. As I eventually sat at the boarding gate, my name was called again. Apparently, my seat was being changed. I never even glanced at the replacement boarding card, I was just so relieved to be still on the plane. Upon entering the plane, I presented my boarding card to the stewardess, and found myself ushered into seat 1F – still a window seat, but now upgraded to first class! That's the only time I've flown first class while on missionary business – and I never even deserved to be flying at all that day!

But again back to the main point: the invitation to pray had come from the airport ground staff – isn't that an amazingly different attitude! In the western world, particularly in Europe, expressions of the Christian faith, specifically, are being driven out of the public arena. As the Christian nurse in the UK found out, this can be a stressful time to be a Christian in the work-place if you're trying to live out your faith. In his second letter to Timothy, the apostle Paul wrote him to "...*realize this, that in the last days difficult times will come*" (2 Timothy 3:1) One Bible version translates it as 'times of stress' – in the last days times of stress will come.

We often, in Christian circles, hear reference being made to 'the last days'. It's important to clarify what the Bible refers to by this expression. Christ brought the last days with him from the time of his first advent. Since the cross we've been living in the last days, biblically-speaking – and, here Paul says, within them, spasmodically at least, we're to expect 'times of stress.' Persecuted Christians in different lands across the globe experience stressful times in extreme ways, but the marginalisation of Christianity within secularised western society is surely also a time of stress – especially in terms of coping with the apathy – and increasingly the hostile resistance against legitimate Christian witness.

It's happened before – that's one thing we can immediately conclude from Paul's writings - so we can learn from history. In facing up to the real challenge of church declension almost two thousand years ago, the very first thing Paul stressed to Timothy was the need to understand the times. And let's be clear, as Paul begins his second biblical letter to Timothy, a real decrease in numbers in the churches has taken place. He writes in 2 Timothy 1:15 about how the whole of Asia had turned away from him. What a contrast to those earlier, glorious days for the Gospel in the very same part of the world. We read in Acts 19:10, that *'all who lived in Asia heard the word of the Lord.'* Years had gone by, and a serious U-turn had taken place: a dramatic reversal of fortunes for the progress of Christianity in the region – a region, by the way, which would correspond with Turkey in our modern world. We've said that there's no doubt we're living in the last days: for the whole Christian era is positioned within them; but also this present time in the West matches the 19-point characterisation that Paul gives at the beginning of 2 Timothy 3 of 'a time of stress' – one that's unfavourable to the progress of the Gospel: *"For men will be lovers of self, lovers of money, boastful, arrogant, revilers, disobedient to parents, ungrateful, unholy, unloving, irreconcilable, malicious gossips, without self-control, brutal, haters of good, treacherous, reckless, conceited, lovers of pleasure rather than lovers of God, holding to a form of godliness, although they have denied its power."*

In the first Bible book of Chronicles we read: *"...of the sons of Issachar, men who understood the times, with knowledge of what Israel should do"* (1 Chronicles 12:32). Like Timothy, and the men of Issachar before him, we need to understand the times we live in: the times, they've been a-changing, so let's try a very brief review of the past few hundred years – just a thumbnail sketch of them in the most relevant terms for our quest concerning the reasons why church growth is difficult. Philosophers have put the past into three categories which they like to call Pre-Modern, Modern and Post-Modern. We'll begin with the 'Pre-Modern' which is the time period from the Middle Ages to the late 17th century. During this time in history, peoples' thinking started with God. There was widespread traditional belief in the supernatural throughout this period.

This was then followed by the period styled as Modern. This was from the late-seventeenth century to the 1970's. During this time, people's thinking began more and more to start with 'I', 'me', and 'my.' Scepticism flourished. This was in part at least the legacy of Rene Descartes. He's the man famous for coining the expression: 'I think, therefore I am.' What was that all about? This was the beginning of the time when people were becoming more and more sceptical in their general outlook, and so he was asking himself: 'What can I be really sure of? It seemed to him that there could be a reason to doubt pretty much everything! In the end, his answer to the question: 'What can I be really sure of?' was to say the only thing he couldn't doubt was that there was a doubter doing the doubting! And that's the background to 'I think therefore I am.' In other words, I'm doing the doubting, so I must exist. So, during this so-called modern era, we find a growing understanding of the physical universe – but it was accompanied by an ever increasing number of people holding to the opinion that we no longer need to believe in God in order to explain our existence.

And so lastly, after the Modern age, we come to the so-called 'Post-Modern' era, which runs from the 1970's to the present day. What's the key idea that characterises this period in which we live? From the 1970's onwards, people came no longer to hold to the idea of absolute, universal truth – but prefer now to think of different truths coexisting. This is why today some claim that totally different ways of reading Scripture are all equally valid, and indeed that different pathways to God exist – in other words, what we have is pluralism on every hand – and not an absolute in sight. Resistance to authority has become more and more widespread too (especially the authority of God's Word, for the Bible has come to be little regarded). Post-modernism rejects the universal and exclusive claims of Christianity. What kind of claims am I talking about? I mean things like the Bible as the exclusive source of special revelation; and the defining moment of a person's life being their acceptance or rejection of the Bible's central message. All these traditional, biblical views are now stumbling blocks to the post-modern mind.

In summary, we, like Timothy, and the men of Issachar before him, need to understand the times we live in, and what's more, we must be people of the book - by which I mean the Bible; for in the same letter in which Paul writes of these things to Timothy, his main emphasis is on appreciating and communicating the Bible. Perhaps that's one main lesson we can learn from how Paul tackled a similar time of numerical decline. It is to reaffirm a passion for the truth of God's Word. We must be bold in our convictions, but at the same time account for the nature of post-modern society in how we go about expressing them. I believe only this can equip us for the challenge facing us today in terms of church growth in the western world. And, we say again, in the western world there's no harder ground for the Gospel than in Western Europe.

3: RECOGNIZING IT'S GOD'S DOING

The Lord in his parable of the Sower famously spoke of four different 'soil' types which represent different degrees of receptivity to the Christian message. In Luke chapter 8, he mentioned the wayside, the rocky ground, the thorny ground and finally the good ground. It would clearly seem that the ground's not good right now in the West - for one thing it's decidedly thorny. Many churches are not growing, at least not numerically.

By contrast, in this chapter we're going to read about an example of real church growth. It's an account of a God-given increase. The apostle Paul in First Corinthians chapter 3 states the principle for all time – that it's God who gives the increase; and, as we'll see, the book of Acts demonstrates how it's the Lord who adds to local church of God fellowship (Acts 2:41-47). So while a lack of numerical church growth rightly ought to concern us, we need to remember that church growth is primarily God's business. That's the angle we begin from as we come now to that example of real church growth we mentioned. I'm taking it from Acts chapter 5...

"But a man named Ananias, with his wife Sapphira, sold a piece of property, and kept back some of the price for himself, with his wife's full knowledge, and bringing a portion of it, he laid it at the apostles' feet. But Peter said, "Ananias, why has Satan filled your heart to lie to the Holy Spirit and to keep back some of the price of the land? While it remained unsold, did it not remain your own? And after it was sold, was it not under your control? Why is it that you have conceived this deed in your heart? You have not lied to men but to God."

And as he heard these words, Ananias fell down and breathed his last; and great fear came over all who heard of it. The young men got up and covered him up, and after carrying him out, they buried him...And great fear came over the whole church, and over all who heard of these things. At the hands of the apostles many signs and wonders were taking place among the people; and they were all with one accord in Solomon's portico. But none of the rest dared to associate with them; however, the people held them in high esteem. And all the more believers in the Lord, multitudes of men and women, were constantly added to their number."
(Acts 5:1-14)

While many believers were being added to their number, that is, to the local Church of God at Jerusalem, we're also told that the people held them in high esteem; and the rest dared not associate with them. We might ask ourselves, 'What produced this divided reaction?' There's little doubt that it was the event described just before this – the summary judgement of God upon Ananias and Sapphira for their covetousness and deceit. It would be natural to read this as saying that the rest of the rich people outside of the church – maybe even those who had personally known Ananias and Sapphira – were deterred by seeing what had happened to this couple; while the general population, hearing of this incident as news of it spread, would also want to keep at a safe distance, having seen the evidence of God's cleansing power against sin among his people and fearing for themselves. So, while the common people held them in respect, even they were counting the cost of discipleship among a people who had a God so near to them.

Overall, those whose interest was only casual would be deterred; whereas those in whose hearts there was a genuine work of God were drawn by the reality of God's power. Adding to the local church was a work of God then, and it takes the same today: it doesn't lie within our power to bring people to the word of truth; but it remains our responsibility to bring the word of truth to people living around us. The bottom line is: there have always been things that will deter people from moving forward with God. So what deters others today? The story's often been told of the little boy being shown around a church building, one which displayed lists of the names of those who had been killed in action in the Great Wars. The guide explained to the boy that all these people had died in the Services – meaning, of course, they'd died in action while serving in the Armed Services. But the youngster misunderstood, and since it was a church building after all, asked if they had died in the morning or the evening church services!

Maybe it's too near the mark to talk of people dying of boredom? Of course, it's true that the individual listening to the sermon shares responsibility for taking an active interest in spiritual things. It's the Holy Spirit's work to make our sermons full of God's convicting power; but surely we've a duty to do our best to communicate in accessible terms with illustrations relevant to the audience. On those occasions when reaching out to the unchurched, we need to show a principled flexibility in our approach. A healthy flexibility will be one that doesn't always insist on doing things the way we've always done them – but, on the other hand, it will still remain loyal to biblical principles. That's why I call it a principled flexibility. We may get rid of nineteenth century traditions; but we're not at any liberty at all to get rid of first century principles (2 Thessalonians 2:15).

But while we talk about the advisability – no, the necessity – to become all things to all men in the way we build bridges with the local communities living around our church halls, let's stress that our reliance can never be on human methods. It's vital that we get to know our neighbourhood as we seek to make social contact at first with our neighbours through offering attractive community activities wherever we can. Mums and Toddler groups, craft classes and computer workshops have all proved to be useful ways of breaking down barriers and getting townsfolk to feel comfortable about coming into the place where the church meets. Then we aim to draw them back again to custom-designed occasions where they'll hear a suitable presentation of the Gospel. But, we say again, our reliance can never be on human methods.

It's reported that the eighteenth-century evangelist Jonathan Edwards was a preacher who read his sermons in an extremely short-sighted fashion and yet multitudes were brought under a conviction which, by all reports, seems to have been very real. So it's not about methods, far less the charisma or eloquence of the speaker. The power lies in the delivery of God's Word. It is this which is living and active, as Hebrews 4:12 reminds us. We shared in the previous chapter how, in order to counter such a time of stress as some of us may also be facing today in parts of the world, Paul makes the Word of God his theme in his second letter to Timothy. He tells Timothy he's to guard it like treasure; and handle accurately the word of truth (2 Timothy 1:12-14; 2:15); hold fast to its authority and inspiration in all matters (3:16); and then preach it urgently (4:2) and with great conviction even when it's inconvenient to do so.

What's more, Paul repeats these things to Timothy with great passion: and in this Post-Modern world we, too, must show a passion– a zeal – for truth! Our earnestness must show that truth is not something to be played around with. What we share is not our mere opinion, but our absolute conviction of what God is saying. It's a wonderful thing to see hearts melting before the raw power of the Word of truth, the whole truth and nothing but the truth!

But when God's at work, so is the Devil, working to oppose the plans and purpose of God. Ever alert to the Devil's attacks, Paul warned Timothy against the snare of the Devil who takes people captive, yes even believers. We see many tragic examples of Satan's, alas, all-too-successful tactics against believers in the New Testament churches of God. It's seen in terms of those who swerved aside from the truth (2 Timothy 2:18-26); and we see it in deceitful workers (2 Corinthians 11:13-15); in strained relationships (James 4:1-7) and in a spirit of insubordination (1 Peter 5:5-8) and even in gossip (1 Timothy 5:13-15). The Devil still attacks in all these ways today, and when we're not healthy, can we really expect to be growing? What this world needs are men and women of God – and to be men and women of God we need to be men and women of the Book – meaning the Bible, of course.

Paul tells Timothy not only to follow the example of his own teaching, but also to follow the example his own godly conduct. Paul lived what he preached, so he could say, *"follow my teaching,* [and my] *conduct..."* (2 Timothy 3:10). Then there follows a description of what cleansed vessels and the Lord's servant should be like – together with a description of what the people of God should be pursuing in terms of righteousness and a pure heart (see 2 Timothy 2:22). If we're really concerned about growth – or the lack of it – don't we need first of all to examine ourselves? Is it possible we've become careless about what we watch on TV; and with how much we drink just so as to be sociable; and about significant fault-lines in our relationships within the churches? Whenever we're jealous, striving to be competitive with one another, whenever we nurse resentments, there's a smile on the face of Satan because we're doing his work and stunting personal, and perhaps church, growth.

4: ENGAGING OUR CULTURE

The early days of Christianity were difficult days. The Roman Empire accused Christians of cannibalism, incest and even atheism in that they didn't respect the pagan gods. Christians were then even more marginalised than they are in much of the western world today. The western media today is generally hostile to Christianity. It is seen as having an 'image' problem – it's viewed as being bigoted against gays and lesbians. Uninformed critics accuse it of demeaning women, and being anti-science. These are all gross distortions, of course, but Christianity is never given the opportunity to explain itself fairly in the media. To do that skilfully at any level within modern society demands that we engage constructively with opposing world views.

A young woman whom I chatted with last summer seemed to have made her own religious omelette, as it were, because the views she advocated seemed to be like a bit of Hinduism, and a bit of Buddhism all thrown together, with a sprinkling of New Age paganism on top. In fact, the only thing missing in her religious world view appeared to be any semblance of biblical Christianity! So often we have to present Christianity in a culture today that's very different from the one in which a previous generation of Christians worked. And a different culture demands a different approach. Then there's the fact that we're up against a different cultural world view in the West compared with parts of the developing world – and again it demands a different approach in which we can almost certainly expect less return for the same hard effort expended. But in another sense this is nothing new. From the Bible book of Acts, here's a little excerpt from the apostle Paul's experience:

"At Lystra a man was sitting who had no strength in his feet, lame from his mother's womb, who had never walked. This man was listening to Paul as he spoke, who, when he had fixed his gaze on him and had seen that he had faith to be made well, said with a loud voice, "Stand upright on your feet". And he leaped up and began to walk. When the crowds saw what Paul had done, they raised their voice, saying in the Lycaonian language, "The gods have become like men and have come down to us." And they began calling Barnabas, Zeus, and Paul, Hermes, because he was the chief speaker." (Acts 14:8-12)

This stands as a classic example of what can so easily happen when we engage with an opposing world view. Paul and Barnabas had given powerful evidence in support of the truth of Christianity. But this evidence, as well as their claims, was totally misinterpreted by the audience because of their own different world view, their own totally different way of understanding things. They, in effect, re-interpreted everything they heard and saw that day. And we need to be alert to the same thing happening to us today – even if it's in much more subtle ways – as when someone from another religious persuasion attaches a totally different meaning to, say the expression 'the Son of God' than the one we intend to convey. But Paul, if we now follow him to Athens, shows us the way to handle this.

Let's read from Acts 17: *"The God who made the world and all things in it, since He is Lord of heaven and earth, does not dwell in temples made with hands...for in Him [that's in God, Paul says] we live and move and exist, as even some of your own poets have said, 'For we also are His children.' Being then the children of God, we ought not to think that the Divine Nature is like gold or silver or stone, an image formed by the art and thought of man."* (Acts17:24-29)

Let's break in there to make the point that this was such a

different type of address from Peter's sermon at Jerusalem in Acts chapter 2. In that very first recorded Christian sermon, Peter quoted chunks of the (Old Testament) Bible and drew on a common religious history. Compared with that, we see Paul's approach was to deliver a different type of address because his evangelising took place in the very different cultural setting of Athens, a pagan centre of learning. And Paul's sermon produced a very different result in terms of the numbers responding – as we can check out as we follow the close of Paul's message at Athens:

"Therefore having overlooked the times of ignorance, God is now declaring to men that all people everywhere should repent, because He has fixed a day in which He will judge the world in righteousness through a Man whom He has appointed, having furnished proof to all men by raising Him from the dead. Now when they heard of the resurrection of the dead, some began to sneer, but others said, "We shall hear you again concerning this." (Acts 17:30-32)

Some have felt Paul made a tactical blunder at Athens; if only he'd begun and ended with Scripture, they say, just as Peter had in Jerusalem. But no, Paul was engaging with a very different worldview, and with people who had little or no exposure to the (Old Testament) Bible. Paul did well to bring the evidence of the natural world to bear, and to quote the literature of his audience's own culture. More than that, Paul had done his research as every preacher should and, in delivering his sermon, he showed an awareness of the worldview of his audience. He knew where they were coming from. Paul models how to research others' views, and how to tactfully help them analyze where these don't stack up.

He demonstrates how to give an effective presentation of the essentials of biblical truth in the most relevant way for a particular audience. For example, perhaps we can pause for a moment to appreciate the way Paul sowed a significant doubt in their minds by asking (and you can find it in Acts 17:29): 'How can you claim the gods made you, if you yourselves are busy making the gods?' He was referring to their idols. This brilliantly exposed the inconsistency of their view. Every worldview outside of the revelation of God's truth, has its inconsistency. We need to help our audience detect this for themselves, as Paul did here. I want to emphasize the value of asking questions, as Paul did. Questions are useful because some will think things through and formulate answers in their own minds later to those questions we ask, and from these they'll not be able to run away even after they've parted company from us.

I've read, but not counted personally, that the Lord Jesus asked some two hundred different questions as recorded in the Gospels. We should learn from the master evangelist. As a faithful preacher, Paul focused his sermon down upon the fact of the resurrection, the reality of Jesus as the coming Judge, and the real need for repentance. I recall a doorstep conversation I had in British Columbia, for an hour perhaps: a conversation where to every Bible-based statement I made, various re-interpretations were given; finally, all I could do was to lay down as a challenge the testable, objective truth of Christianity which is found in the resurrection of Jesus Christ (see 1 Corinthians 15:14). As with these Athenians two thousand years ago, we have to let the modern sceptic grapple honestly with the best supported fact of history, as expert historians and lawyers have called it.

The 'Alpha course' approach (as distinct from its content in parts) - the same as is used also in the Christianity Explored course – is all about being non-threatening, as well as being about showing a preparedness to listen and engage in discussion regardless of the views of others. I believe this is why it's been successful in a post-modern world. After listening and engaging, like Paul at Athens, the vital next step is to help them to process for themselves the weaknesses of divergent views, all the while feeding in relevant biblical truth little by little, line upon line. And if we do our homework, we can be ready to answer the same questions which always come back at us. I firmly believe the popularity of this approach in recent times in the West is because it's an approach which recognizes that hammering away with a heavily-laden Bible sermon is no longer likely to be as effective as one which shares truth in a relevant and illustrative way and then solicits others' opinions as a starting point for engaging in informed discussion.

In other words, it's an approach that recognizes, if you like, that we're in an Athens-type environment today in the West, and not in a Jerusalem-type environment. But the basic problem remains this: for us the Bible is of supreme authority; while for them it has little weight. For us there is but one way of salvation and service, but they're conditioned to be tolerant and respectful of many ways. What can we do? First be passionate about our own convictions. Then listen, engage, show genuine interest, try to understand, and begin to sow doubt by asking questions. Then, as appropriate, gently present the evidence for Christianity.

And don't we need to extend the Alpha-type approach, beyond dealing with the debate over God's existence, and the uniqueness of Christ? Just as all religious paths don't lead to God; neither are all biblical interpretations equally plausible. So we need to engage with those who say 'well, some say this is right and others that's right, so that justifies us in choosing whichever happens to be most convenient for us.' Why, for example, can't we passionately advocate the model of church government that's most consistent with the glorious truth of the Body of Christ? Why can't we thrill to persuasively show which understanding of worship best explains Hebrews chapters 9, 10 and 11?

5: IDENTIFYING KEY FACTORS

I think it would be fair to say that Paul's focus was not so much on growing churches but on achieving healthy churches comprised of mature disciples. Paul expresses what might pass today for a mission statement in the first chapter of his letter to the Christians in Colossae: *"We proclaim Him [Christ], admonishing every man and teaching every man with all wisdom, so that we may present every man complete in Christ"* (Colossians 1:28).

Having said that, a healthy church will surely be one that's undergoing healthy development or growth. A number of years ago an extensive study was conducted by an organization to identify the key factors which were contributing to the growth of evangelical churches. It identified eight factors which growth was shown to be sensitive to. The results seem plausible – for the simple reason that we can fairly easily identify these factors as being in operation among the New Testament churches of God. And the factors were:

Empowering leadership – of which we get this example: *"...brethren, select from among you seven men of good reputation, full of the Spirit* *and of wisdom, whom we may put in charge of this task."* (Acts 6:3) There the apostles shared out responsibilities through delegating and involving others in specific ministries. That's empowering leadership. Then there's...

Effective small group activities – of which we get this example: *"...they came to their own company, and reported all that the chief priests and the elders had said unto them"* (Acts 4:23). This was the time when Peter and John, after having been apprehended by the authorities, were finally released. We're told that they returned to their own company (Revised Version Bible) - which seems to imply that the Church of God in Jerusalem in those days was so numerous that it wasn't practical for them all to meet together in one place, so there were several companies of believers comprising the one church in that city. This would allow many more of the different spiritual gifts of the many believers to be utilized; and allow more personal involvement and mentoring. Might we not see in this the beginning of the principle of smaller group activities? Then there's...

Passionate spirituality - something commanded of believers by the apostle Paul when he said that they should be *"...fervent in spirit; serving the Lord"* (Romans 12:11). And alongside passionate spirituality, there's the need for...

Loving relationships – as demonstrated by the well-known words: *"And if I have the gift of prophecy, and know all mysteries and all knowledge; and if I have all faith, so as to remove mountains, but have not love, I am nothing"* (1 Corinthians 13:2). And the character of that love is described fully in the remainder of that wonderful chapter. If our church relationships lived up to all those qualities, our churches certainly would be healthy places. Then there's...

Fervent worship & prayer – which we can glimpse here: *"when they had prayed, the place was shaken wherein they were gathered together; and they were all filled with the Holy Ghost, and they spake the word of God with boldness."* (Acts 4:31) How's that for fervent prayer – and then there's...

Organization that works – of which here's an example: *"Since we have heard that some of our number to whom we gave no instruction have* *disturbed you with their words, unsettling your souls, it seemed good to us, having become of one mind, to select men to send to you with our beloved Barnabas and Paul, men who have risked their lives for the name of our Lord Jesus Christ. Therefore we have sent Judas and Silas, who themselves will also report the same things by word of mouth"* (Acts 15:24-27). Here care was taken to communicate very clearly, the unity of mind in decision-making which had been arrived at by the leadership – a leadership which was throughout all the churches. That's an outstanding example of Spirit-controlled organization. Then there's...

Gift-oriented ministry – as we read: *"And He gave some as apostles, and some as prophets, and some as evangelists, and some as pastors and teachers, for the equipping of the saints for the work of service.* (Ephesians 4:11-12)" And finally, after gift-oriented ministry, there's …

Needs-based evangelism – of which the greatest example is surely that of the Lord talking to the woman at the well in Samaria, as found in John's Gospel, chapter 4. From the woman's need of natural water, the Lord led on to her deeper need of living water. It's good when we can be in touch with our neighbourhood via community projects. These things are increasingly useful as pre-evangelistic steps. If we've got all these quality factors present which were once typical of New Testament Christian experience in the first ever Churches of God, then ours should be a healthy local church.

But nationally (such as in a country like the U.K.) we hear that interest in attending church services in many parts is in serious decline. What can we do? One study boldly announced that there are answers in the face of declining church attendance. The answers it shared were practical:

Be welcoming; get the building to say 'hello!' it advised. Some of our church premises are none too inviting, frankly. Try to look at them again through the eyes of a newcomer. Or, could it be, that if someone comes along and expresses a contrary view, we react with outspoken condemnation of the views they express? If we're convinced what they say is not biblical, we do have to respond, but there's a tactful way to go about it, surely. We need to meet people where they are, but also be undeterred in our vision to bring them with us all the way into the full-blooded conviction of what being an authentic biblical Church of God is all about.

Act generally as though you expect 'outsiders' to come in, was a second piece of advice. It may be that we're so unaccustomed to receiving visitors into our church services that we make an embarrassing fuss of them.

Thirdly, the study recommended that we **preach about things people talk about**. For example, the Lord had a lot to say about money...well that's certainly (pardon the pun) common currency among topics which interest people. We can so easily talk at people, about things they don't connect with, in language that's inaccessible to them; all the while showing ourselves to be uncomfortable in their company. **Make the kids happy and they'll bring their parents along** was a fourth piece of advice. And finally, it said: **Worship like you really mean it**. It's hard to argue with that.

Another study ("The Tide is Running Out"), made similar points: when it too advised: **Provide inspiring worship; address the real needs of the community; aim to be welcoming to outsiders; present the historic claims of the Bible; and teach about God's love and the work of Christ with clarity** – and we might add: **present distinctive truth with 'a wow factor'**. When we do these things, we may hope to see active individuals within the church make contacts outside the church; and these contacts then become attenders at church services. Some of these attenders hopefully will then go on to become regular attenders. And some regular attenders will then be added to the church, and newly added individuals themselves will in time become active, and the cycle begins to repeat when these new active individuals in turn start to make fresh contacts...

Sometimes the challenge of growth is less daunting when we see it broken down into single steps, each do-able with the Lord's gracious help. May God indeed give the increase!

6: SOWING THE SEED

The first verses in the Bible show that God, our Creator, is a God of growth. *"God said, 'Let the earth bring forth grass, the herb that yields seed'....And the earth brought forth grass, the herb that yields seed according to its kind, and the tree that yields fruit, whose seed is in itself according to its kind. And God saw that it was good."* (Genesis 1:11-12)

So straightaway in the Bible, we're introduced to the idea of things growing from seed. This is God's way for things to grow. Even the first mention of the promised Saviour is one which refers to Him as "the seed of the woman" (Genesis 3:15). This principle of growth from seed is one we meet when we search our Bible for the secrets of church growth. The growth of local Christians, in local churches, is described for us in the language of seeds and seedlings - things which require planting and watering as well as careful nurturing, pruning and protection. It's only right and proper that we should look into our Bibles for help on this practical and challenging subject of church growth, for the Bible is the 'Word of life'.

The Word of God itself is the spiritual seed that brings about the new life of each Christian in the first place. Far in advance of modern science, the words of Jesus Christ established the reality of a seed going into the earth and dying in order that it might become fruitful and multiply through vigorous growth (John 12:24). Yet even before that fact was known, sowing and reaping had become the natural rhythms of growth as harnessed for the supply of our daily food. Directly against that background, in the fields around a town of Samaria, Jesus Christ gave this description of evangelical growth: *"Do you not say, 'There are still four months and then comes the harvest'? Behold, I say to you, lift up your eyes and look at the fields, for they are already white for harvest! And he who reaps receives wages, and gathers fruit for eternal life, that both he who sows and he who reaps may rejoice together. For in this the saying is true: 'One sows and another reaps.' I sent you to reap that for which you have not labored; others have labored, and you have entered into their labor'"* (John 4:35-38).

Jesus clearly drew a contrast between sowing and reaping. It's as if He positively wanted us to realize that the work of evangelism is as much about sowing as it is about reaping. In the midst of the joy of the spiritual harvest that would be reaped that day when the Good News of the Saviour came through the woman to the townspeople, Jesus spoke up there and then for the earlier work of nameless individuals who had already sown - maybe years before. The first obvious lesson for us is not to overlook the sowing, for there can be no reaping without sowing. The work of sowing is indispensable, even though it doesn't carry the same thrill as the joy of reaping - when the results are obvious, and the labour brings its own immediate reward.

I suppose, we'd all much rather reap than sow, but as Jesus sent out His disciples to reap, He reminded them that others had done the hard work to prepare the ground. It's rare for the painstaking work of sowing to be highly acclaimed - especially nowadays when the world tries to condition us to value only those things that provide immediate results. But that day back in John chapter four the Lord mentioned – and appreciated - the work done by others before the disciples ever came near the town where they'd reap that spiritual harvest.

In fact, when He said: 'Others have done the hard work', He was really putting the contribution of His own disciples into some perspective. What they were going to be involved in that day was easy compared to the work of sowing that had been done there in the past. Talk about reaping the benefits of the hard work of others! Sometimes we want to see immediate results for our witnessing. Praise the Lord, there are times when that happens; but isn't it because someone else has sown a seed, maybe over years of effort? And so now they have *"been born again, not of corruptible seed but incorruptible through the word of God which lives and abides forever"* (1 Peter 1:23).

The Lord has called each of us, every single believer, to be His witnesses: to sow the seed of His Word in the lives of people all around us. Hopefully, then, there are people we know, and can relate to, into whose lives we're trying to have a consistent spiritual input. They may be family members, including our own children of course, but perhaps they are colleagues, friends, neighbours - someone, anyone about whom the Lord has touched our heart. We keep them on our regular prayer list, and we look for opportunities to 'sow a seed' in a very natural way when in conversation with them. A little experience teaches us that it's not usually helpful to say too much all at once, unless there's an obvious hunger for what we're saying; so that we're just responding to questions. More usually, we'll cultivate a relationship with people we expect to see regularly, although we must try to avoid the danger of never actually getting round to saying anything that's too directly evangelical! In this way, sowing is bound up with the process of preparing the ground for what we say.

This surely reminds us of the famous parable told by Jesus about the Sower in Matthew's Gospel. *"Therefore hear the parable of the sower: When anyone hears the word of the kingdom, and does not understand it, then the wicked one comes and snatches away what was sown in his heart. This is he who received seed by the wayside. But he who received the seed on stony places, this is he who hears the word and immediately receives it with joy; yet he has no root in himself, but endures only for a while. For when tribulation or persecution arises because of the word, immediately he stumbles. Now he who received seed among the thorns is he who hears the word, and the cares of this world and the deceitfulness of riches choke the word, and he becomes unfruitful. But he who received seed on the good ground is he who hears the word and understands it, who indeed bears fruit and produces: some a hundredfold, some sixty, some thirty.'"* (Matthew 13:18-23)

The sower realizes that a certain type of soil is necessary for a fruitful response from the seed sown. If someone we're witnessing to seems unresponsive, it may be that their situation corresponds to one of the soil deficiencies that Jesus spoke about. They may be distracted, for example, by various pressures at that moment in time. A little wisdom might suggest that we find a practical way to help them out, or maybe simply wait until a better opportunity presents itself. In either case, please be assured: you've not failed at reaping, you've been sowing. That's something different, and just as important. God's Law teaches us to 'love our neighbour', and that 'great command' of loving our neighbour is totally consistent with the 'great commission' of directly going and making disciples. For, as C.S. Lewis once said, 'Love is the great apologetic'. Attitudes and actions which really show the love of Christ help to overcome resistance to God's Good News.

Going and making disciples is our mission statement; surely one of the greatest mission statements ever given. As individuals, and as local churches, we won't lose our focus on this great mission while we feel the Lord burdening our souls in prayer for those around us who are lost without the knowledge of Jesus Christ as their Saviour. Don't give up on 'going' and 'sowing' - for there's no quicker way to the harvest. In sowing - this essential aspect of evangelism – we're to continue to make God's Word available to those around us, both privately and publicly; as individuals and collectively; and to continue even when the response seems small or non-existent.

In writing his Bible letter to Timothy, Paul really stressed that hard work and skill is required of us. It takes skill to see the opportunity and share something in a relevant way. Like the hard-working farmer who sows his fields, we're to sow in unwearying toil, waiting on the Holy Spirit to create spiritual interest and conviction. That's something, of course, which He alone can do.

7: REAPING THE HARVEST

'*G*o *into all the world and make disciples, baptizing them in the name of the Father, the Son, and the Holy Spirit, teaching them to observe all things* [He has] *commanded* [us].*"* All the seeds of growth are there. As a mission statement it's totally focused on growth. Our purpose is to be involved in this process. In the last chapter, we were emphasizing only the first part of that commission - the 'going' part – when the Lord said 'Go into all the world'. Now we'd like to think through the process of growth after the sowing has been done. It's worth saying that the spiritual harvest God is looking for isn't limited to others coming to know His salvation only. The Lord in the parable of the Sower spoke of different levels of fruitfulness: thirtyfold, sixtyfold and even a hundredfold. We can't help but think of this harvest in terms of disciple-making, believer's baptism and fulfilling all of the Lord's teaching for our Christian lives. The measure of response can vary, the extent of fruitfulness can differ.

Let's begin again with the Lord's visit to the well outside the Samaritan town. It was in the fields around that town of Samaria that Jesus Christ gave this commentary on evangelical growth: *"Do you not say, 'There are still four months and then comes the harvest'? Behold, I say to you, lift up your eyes and look at the fields, for they are already white for harvest! And he who reaps receives wages, and gathers fruit for eternal life, that both he who sows and he who reaps may rejoice together. For in this the saying is true: 'One sows and another reaps.' I sent you to reap that for which you have not labored; others have labored, and you have entered into their labors'"* (John 4:35-38).

The starting reference to the harvest being four months away probably had to do with the natural harvest of the crop in the nearby fields. Yet wasn't Jesus watching the people streaming out of the town to meet Him, when He spoke of the fields being already white for harvesting? Surely He was. The joy of the reaper would be known in town that very day. A spiritual harvest was gathered in as the townspeople first believed the woman's witness and then heard the preaching of the Lord Himself. But what if it's a long time since we personally knew the joy of reaping in the field of evangelism? What if it's some time since our local church shared the joy of reaping even a small spiritual harvest? In some parts of the world, particularly the western world at this point in history, there's a longing to see a revival, a revival such as we read about taking place in past centuries in those same areas where response now seems to be so small.

Imagine a farmer going out into his fields to demand a harvest! That's ridiculous, isn't it? He's got to sow his seed first, and then wait, before there can ever be a harvest. He can't just have a harvest when he wants one; and he'll never have one at all, unless he's prepared to sow, and then wait for the right time in the natural cycle of things. Weren't these revivals also preceded by the long, hard work of sowing? The names we associate with revivals are not the names of those who did all the advance hard work. Yet one day these nameless workers will get due recognition and their full share of the joy - just as the Lord paid tribute to the nameless sowers who had laboured in and around this town of Samaria mentioned in John chapter four.

The timescale of reaping is very short compared with the length of time for sowing and waiting. There's a time to reap. It could be, that where you're working, it's not time for reaping, but it's time for sowing. There's a time to reap and there's a time to sow. We were thinking about that in the previous chapter. But what we now want to move on to emphasize is that we shouldn't lose the expectation of reaping. The Lord's command to His disciples was, and remains, 'go and make disciples'. That 'going' must be going out just as in the picture of the farmer going out into his field to sow the seed. But the object in view is the 'making of disciples', and must take us into the activity of reaping, even if it's only a small harvest. If we sow (certainly if we do it wisely by God's help) we expect to reap.

My young daughter sowed some sunflower seeds in a small pot filled with soil and placed them on the kitchen window-sill. Every day, for a while, she looked to see if anything was happening yet. She knows what to expect this time, for she did the same last year. With some watering and the sunlight which streams in through the window, she didn't have too long to wait before a thin green shoot became visible. Once transplanted into the garden, it should grow up into a strong tall stem which, in time, will dwarf her and support its golden sunflower. She sowed her seeds in expectation, and then just left things to happen by themselves - apart from mum watering them while they were indoors!

That reminds me of the farmer the Lord spoke of in Mark's Gospel when He pictured the Kingdom of God in this way: *"A man scatters seed on the ground. Night and day, whether he sleeps or gets up, the seed sprouts and grows, though he does not know how. All by itself the soil produces corn - first the stalk, then the ear, then the full grain in the ear. As soon as the grain is ripe, he puts the sickle to it, because the harvest has come"* (Mark 4:26-29). The farmer sows his seed and there's nothing more that he can do until the result of that sowing, the growth, has become obvious. Untill then, it's the work of God while the farmer sleeps. It's God who gives the increase. It's to Him we must look in expectant prayer after we've done our bit of sowing. The God who bathes the farmer's fields in sunshine, is the God who enlightens the person in whom a Scriptural seed has been sown. *"For it is the God who commanded light to shine out of darkness, who has shone in our hearts to give the light of the knowledge of the glory of God in the face of Jesus Christ."* (2 Corinthians 4:6) Only the God of creation can create new life and cause it to develop. As we wait for this, we pray patiently for the showers of blessing. Even as *"the farmer waits for the precious fruit of the earth, waiting patiently for it until it receives the early and latter rain"* (James 5:7).

"For the earth which drinks in the rain that often comes upon it, and bears herbs useful for those by whom it is cultivated, receives blessing from God" (Hebrews 6:7). Sometimes we sing, 'mercy drops round us are falling, but for the showers we plead'. We plead with God for the showers, as He puts into our hearts the desire to ask fervently for it. God is the sovereign God. He's sovereign in the bestowing of His blessings, and sovereign in the timing of them. It will happen as His purposes ripen in the life of some individual with whom we've had dealings. Of course, we long for crowds to respond, and remember how it's recorded of the Lord Jesus that He *"went about all the cities and villages, teaching in their synagogues, preaching the gospel of the kingdom...among the people. But when He saw the multitudes, He was moved with compassion for them, because they were weary and scattered, like sheep having no shepherd. Then He said to His disciples, "The harvest truly is plentiful, but the laborers are few. Therefore pray the Lord of the harvest to send out laborers into His harvest"'* (Matthew 9:35-38).

We, too, must not wait for people to come to us. We've also to make contact with the people in the communities in which we live, and who live around our church halls. It may be that we will use community-related good works which serve as a genuine starting-point. Such good works hold the promise of reaping, where it says: *"Let us not grow weary while doing good, for in due season we shall reap if we do not lose heart"* (Galatians 6:9). There's nothing like everyday contact with the people around us to impress upon us the emptiness of a life without Christ, and to move us, too, with compassion that expresses itself in pleading prayer to the sovereign Lord of the Harvest that we may be enabled to draw alongside some and become active in discipling them.

8: PLANTING THE SEEDLINGS

Near the beginning of the Bible, we can read that God *"planted a garden eastward in Eden, and there He put the man whom He had formed"* (Genesis 2:8). This garden was a special place, separate from the common field around. The Garden of Eden was, above all, a place of the divine presence. We read of God coming down to walk with the man in the garden in the cool of the day. It was a place of purpose, too, for God gave to Adam the pleasant duty of tending, cultivating and keeping it (Genesis 2:15). Then, in the most tragic of all ways, we discover by the Bible's third chapter that this garden was also a place where actions would be judged.

The garden was a prepared place, entirely suitable for man to flourish and develop in communion with God. It contained fruit for nourishment and in it was the head of the river that met its needs and those of the land around. The Garden of Eden was something that owed its origin to God. It was marked out as different from its surroundings. It was God who put people inside it, as distinct from them being on the outside. It was a place where the presence of God was known in a very special way. In addition, it was a place of service with God-given duties, suited to God-given abilities and gifts. It was a place of responsibility and privilege, and also of discipline. This was a place designed to nourish relationships with God; while meeting needs both inside and outside.

Do any of these features strike you as familiar? They should do, if you belong to a Biblical church! When the apostle Paul wrote to the New Testament Church of God at Corinth, he called them God's cultivated land (1 Corinthians 3:9 Revised Version Margin) - with all we've been saying in the back of his mind, too, I'm sure. That church, like its sister churches, was 'of God' as to its origin; and its character marked it out as different from the surrounding moral looseness of the busy seaport. God's power had transformed some of the city's inhabitants and brought them and added them to the local church there. God's presence was indeed known among them, so that there could be talk of them being God's temple. To the believers gathered together there, Paul had a lot to say about spiritual gifts, used in serving God. Paul used his authority as an apostle to judge them, too, and called on the church itself to exercise discipline, even to the extent of expelling from its number someone who was behaving in an immoral way.

So the Church of God at Corinth, in all these ways, was like the first garden to be planted. The Corinthians were the context for, if not the object of, Paul's labour: *"I planted"* (3:6a; 3:9b). Seedlings should be together: not surrounded by hostile weeds but alongside other seedlings which can then be given systematic 'watering' (3:6b). This illustration agrees with the teaching example of Acts 2:47, where the new believers were added 'together', forming, as it were, seedplots of growing seedlings.

These Corinthians being addressed were now *'the planting of the Lord'* (Isaiah 61:3; cp. 1 Corinthians 9:7; Genesis 2:8). How was Paul able to bring about growing gardens in places like Corinth, which were so sinful that they were, if you like, spiritual wildernesses? Let's see if we can discover practical hints from Paul's way of working – practical hints for planting churches that continue to grow, or at least, the transplanting of individuals into an already growing church of God. The first thing that strikes us is how Paul saw God's directing hand in his everyday circumstances. Someone has said - and I think it's true - that being visionary isn't all to do with having wonderful high-flown ideas. More usually, real vision in our mission work for the Lord is about seeing opportunities in some quite ordinary situations.

Take, for example, the time recorded at the beginning of Acts 18 when Paul arrived in Corinth. He soon settled in with a couple of people who were of the same tent-making occupation as he was. What an opportunity it must have been for Paul as they handled the tent cloth together - an opportunity to teach them how to handle the Word of God too! I've no doubt Paul made the connection. In one of his Bible letters he talks about 'cutting straight' the word of truth (2 Timothy 2:15). By the end of the same chapter Paul's tent-making companions were not only making straight cuts in their cloth, but they were cutting the word of truth straight for themselves, and even more than that: they were helping others - like someone called Apollos - to divide it correctly as well (Acts 18:26). It's a very practical point, for often the people we're most effective at reaching out to are people most like ourselves - with the same profession maybe, or with family of a similar age and at school together.

Vision is seeing the opportunity for mission in the normal run of life. From such contacts, as we cultivate the relationship, God can use us to be instrumental in bringing new seedlings into his local garden. At Corinth, Paul used another tactic which had often served him well. He made himself known in the local synagogue. As he reasoned with these folks who were already in the habit of thinking and talking about God, he encountered opposition to the teaching he brought, but in the divisions that arose he was able to discern those in whose hearts there was a further work of God going on, and these were the people he followed through on, forming a smaller separated group when that became necessary. Perhaps, the synagogues were obvious places, but in Philippi, Paul scouted out a spot down by the river where people gathered for prayer. Once again he was being directed to where there were those whose hearts the Spirit had already been preparing (Acts 16).

If we have the same desire to find spiritually prepared hearts, will God not direct us too? What I always find impressive about Paul was his adaptability. He reminded the Corinthians that to the Jews he became as a Jew; to the weak he became weak; in fact he became all things to all men. There's not a hint of compromise here, only the pure motivation that he might by all means save some (1 Corinthians 9:22). What a singular focus on the Christian mission! The approach, the method and the tactics were all secondary (although we can be sure they were all Biblical). The key point was that they were all made to serve the same purpose of winning the lost. Mission must win out over method. Conviction, drawing and saving is all God's work, of course; but God employs us as His instruments, expecting us to work hard, act worthily and to become skilful with whatever approaches are effective within our culture and society. If we find ourselves living in an age of informality or in a very visual age, then the Spirit of God can work with the grain of our society in these things, as we bathe it all in prayer while attempting to be adaptable.

Inevitably there will be growing pains. It would not have been necessary to explain the meaning of the word 'setback' to Paul. He knew what it was to be thrown out, or dragged before the magistrates; but perhaps what was even harder to take, he also experienced times when co-workers seemed to lose the vision and give up. Some he had seen come to faith later turned away. Paul was never one to be deterred. I'm sure, like me, there have been times when you've been glad to reread Paul's verdict: *"Let us not grow weary while doing good, for in due season we shall reap if we do not lose heart"* (Galatians 6:9). That was borne out in his personal experience as we read of it in our Bibles. We mustn't allow hindrances to deter us; often they are a sure sign that we're moving in God's plan. For whenever God is truly at work through His Spirit, we can be sure that

Satan will be active in trying to oppose whatever we're doing. Causing us to be discouraged is one of the methods he uses.

When the Lord Jesus said 'Go' into the world around us, He never set any limits, so we need to be ambitious. I appreciated the spiritual ambition that came over in a recent report I was reading from sister churches in Africa. In moving into an adjacent area they had enlisted the support of pioneer-minded brothers and sisters to give of their time - some a week, some a month – that they might mobilize to become a team of temporary residents in that area. Full-time workers gave leadership and this team gave themselves to prayer and organized rallies. Those who were able committed themselves to long-term follow-through. New churches are still planted in this way as an outreach from a neighbouring established church. By God's help, ambition can be kept alive even when we plough a lonely furrow in ground that's hard, where nothing seems to grow quickly.

Allowing ourselves to be Spirit-directed to people with an existing spiritual openness, by ensuring our methods are adaptable, and by overcoming setbacks, we can hold on to the boldness of our spiritual ambition to make friendly contact with people like ourselves. Then we can bring them together to form a small cell group, where its warmth and informality help disciples to be trained, and from which ultimately a church may be planted and grow.

9: WATERING THE CROPS

There are many wrong ideas about what church growth is. Growth is not one congregation expanding at the expense of others. It's not the drawing power of an attractive personality, nor adopting some current fad or fashion in order to draw the curious and thrill-seekers (the sort of people that the apostle Paul memorably described as those with 'itching ears'). Christian experience was never designed to be something akin to the market-place, where consumers 'taste' and 'browse' without any Biblical commitment. For growth to be real growth it has to be Biblical growth: growth that's in and through the Word.

Recently when I was reading Paul's second pastoral letter to Timothy, I was very forcibly struck by just how contemporary its message is. Paul was writing at a time when numbers were declining in a large area of the early New Testament fellowship of churches of God, for he wrote, *"all those in Asia have turned away from* [him]*"* (2

Timothy 1:15). Even though there had been this drop in numbers way back in the first century, Paul was still able to be forward-looking as he prepared to hand the baton of ministry over to Timothy. What is it that seems to make Paul's letter sound right up to date? Two things seem to stand out in this 'state of the nation' message to Timothy that came from the pen of Paul.

First of all, there's a tremendous emphasis on the Word of God throughout the whole of this second letter. Timothy was told to *"hold fast the pattern of sound words"* (2 Timothy 1:13); and *"to rightly divide the word of truth"* (2 Timothy 2:15). He was told that he must *"preach the Word"* (2 Timothy 4:2), for, after all, *"all Scripture is given by inspiration of God"* (2 Timothy 3:16). It was in this letter, too, that Paul compared Christian service to the labour of a hard-working farmer (2 Timothy 2:6). Among Paul's favourite words were those used here - words which stress the strong exertion required in Christian service. The work of a farmer is hard work, and even more so in those earlier times when there was little mechanical help. Paul wanted to get the point across that Christian service is really hard work. There should be such a thing as a 'Christian work ethic'. No one should ever get the foolish notion from reading Paul's letters that the world owed them a living.

Today, modern trends swirl around us which would seem to challenge the very things which Paul emphasizes here. For isn't there a tendency to soft-pedal serious study of the Word of God, while at the same time there's so much talk of the supernatural that energetic toil in service seems unspiritual? But God has joined these things together. We have already thought of the local church as a garden, and anyone who has to care for a garden knows the hard work that's involved. Like farming, gardening is also hard work. One of the main tasks in gardening has a vital spiritual counterpart. Plants need watering, especially when they're tender or have just been transplanted. Isaiah, in his Bible prophecy, pictured the Lord Jesus entering human experience in this world as *'a tender plant...out of dry ground'* (Isaiah 53:2).

The world is dry ground for a Christian. There's nothing in the world's way of thinking and behaving that can give any refreshment to the Christian life. There's no nourishment for the soul there. Yet Isaiah's messages also contained a promise for the people of God then. For those who followed in God's way, the promise was: *"The LORD will guide you continually, and satisfy your soul in drought, and strengthen your bones; you shall be like a watered garden"* (Isaiah 58:11). There again we have the picture of how God sees those who follow His way as being like a watered garden. The source of water, or watering, is the Word of God itself. Only that which brought us life can sustain the life we have in Christ through faith. In Ephesians, Paul described it as *"the water of the Word"* (5:26).

In the watered gardens that were the New Testament churches of God, it's easy to see that there were structured, accessible Bible-teaching programmes for growth. Certainly that was the Lord's plan, for think of the time *"when they had eaten breakfast, Jesus said to Simon Peter, 'Simon, son of Jonah, do you love Me more than these?' He said to Him, 'Yes, Lord; You know that I love You.' He said to him, 'Feed My lambs.' He said to him again a second time, 'Simon, son of Jonah, do you love Me?' He said to Him, 'Yes, Lord; You know that I love You.' He said to him, 'Tend My sheep.' He said to him the third time, 'Simon, son of Jonah, do you love Me?' Peter was grieved because He said to him the third time, 'Do you love Me?' And he said to Him, 'Lord, You know all things; You know that I love You.' Jesus said to him, 'Feed My sheep.'"* (John 21:15-17)

Jesus began by emphasizing feeding and also ended with it. In between, He talked about 'tending'. He was outlining the scope of Christian pastoral ministry. The main point for us is to see that it begins and ends with the feeding of the Word of God - or we could just as rightly say, the watering of the Word of God. The pre-eminence of the teaching and application of the Word is therefore something that should be a marked feature in pastoral ministry. Recently, I came across the results of a survey that had been carried out on what were described as growing churches. One of the claims made was that among the features of growing churches was this: that they were notable for their cross-centred teaching - teaching that was with clarity and conviction - and in the demonstration of the Holy Spirit's power, of course.

I can't vouch for that report's finding, but one thing I can say is that it doesn't surprise me in the least. You'd have to expect that result from the Bible's own teaching, as we've seen. The teaching of God's Word is all bound up with pictures of refreshment and growth. Moses said: *"Hear, O earth, the words of my mouth. Let my teaching drop as the rain, my speech distill as the dew, as raindrops on the tender herb, and as showers on the grass"* (Deuteronomy 32:1-2). It was Isaiah who spoke from God when he said: *"For as the rain comes down, and the snow from heaven, and do not return there, but water the earth, and make it bring forth and bud, that it may give seed to the sower and bread to the eater, so shall My word be that goes forth from My mouth"* (Isaiah 55:10-11).

In these varied references to water as in the dew and snow, the Word of God is consistently being pictured as providing the watering that's necessary for growth. In the Old Testament, God had shown the tenderness of His character as being like that of a Gardener busy working in the vineyard that was His people Israel. He said, *"I will water it every moment: lest any hurt it, I will keep it night and day"* (Isaiah 27:3). In the New Testament, and at Corinth of which we've thought before, the Bible teacher known as Apollos fulfilled the task of bringing the stimulating Word to those newly planted in the Church of God there. Paul said: *"I planted...Apollos watered."* The clarity of teaching presentations from God's Word will always be a key factor in moving people from being regular attenders to finding their place in the local church. All teaching that's Bible-based doesn't have to be done in a formal church setting, of course, even when the aim is quite definitely to arrive at church growth.

In fact, in Europe there are those who have claimed for some time that informal house Bible studies seem to be the most effective approach in the early stages of spiritual growth. The mood for productive interaction can often be set by offering refreshments, and possibly after an introduction using visual media, there can be open, friendly discussion with the opportunity for real sharing of God's

Word at a basic level. Then, just as the Lord Jesus spoke of providing for the sheep as well as the lambs, and just as the apostle Paul described more advanced Bible teaching as 'spiritual meat', compared to the 'spiritual milk', we can progress gradually to more advanced discipleship teaching. Appropriate teaching that's accessible for each level of maturity: that's the ideal to be seen in a healthy growing church.

What could be more conducive to promoting growth than having preaching and teaching programs where God's Word is revealed in messages that are crafted by the Spirit's help and presented with the same Spirit's power - clear, convincing presentations of God's truth that are Christ-centred, Bible-based and life-oriented? That's teaching for growth! That's learning that lives!

10: CULTIVATING THE LAND

W e've been thinking about God as a God of growth; and of how He arranges for the growth of things from seed. It's the good seed of God's Word itself that brings about each new Christian life. It's also God's Word which continues to water or nourish it. The Bible has given us the illustration of these 'seedlings' being planted together in a church environment, which it compares to land undergoing cultivation - a garden situation, just as at the very beginning.

The Garden of Eden was something that owed its origin to God. It was marked out as different from its surroundings. It was God who put people inside it, as distinct from them being on the outside. It was a place where the presence of God was known in a very special way. In addition, it was a place of service with God-given duties, suited to God-given abilities and gifts. It was a place of responsibility and privilege, and also of discipline. This was a place designed to nourish relationships with God; it was a place where needs were met. All these features of Eden's garden exactly illustrate the characteristics to be found in a Biblical church of God. In Genesis chapter two, we're told that God gave Adam the duty of cultivating the garden. Any garden needs to be tended and cultivated if it's not to become fallow ground. The same thing applies to a church of God.

So, to take an example of a New Testament church of God, how was church life at Corinth being cultivated? We start with the matter of being rooted and grounded in Christ's love (see Ephesians 3:17) - of which Paul wrote famously in chapter thirteen of his first letter to them. Cultivating a real sense of the love of Christ will make for a welcoming as well as a healthy environment. Can anything be more attractive than the love of God? Then we read a lot in Paul's first letter to Corinth about the use of spiritual gifts, and it should be a reminder to us all that we're all gifted. Every believer has been specially endowed with a gift from God, so we should all aim to find out how the Lord wants us to serve Him, for none of us are to remain spectators. We shouldn't allow our gift to lie fallow, but we should cultivate it. It's interesting to note that the Bible associates fallow ground not only with disuse and inactivity - it also connects fallow ground with waste, poverty, and injustice: together with neglect of spiritual duties and a failure to seek the Lord (Proverbs 13:23; Jeremiah 4:3; Hosea 10:12). Churches of God were never intended to become like that, and so the work of cultivation must take place there.

It was also in that first letter Paul wrote to the church of God at Corinth that the apostle Paul described the church as God's cultivated land (see 1 Corinthians 3:9 Revised Version Margin). Yet this was a garden with problems, a garden with weeds – and we discover what makes for effective tending of God's tilled land by looking at the correction that the Spirit provided through Paul's letter. In a bustling seaport like Corinth visitors wouldn't be unusual. So people came in to observe the church services at Corinth. Some of these visitors may well have been contacts of folks in the church.

They could even have been invited by neighbours to come along.

How disappointing to those making the contacts - and doing the inviting – if whenever these friends showed up they got a very unfavourable impression of Christianity! At one point Paul said: *"if all prophesy, and an unbeliever or an uninformed person comes in, he is convinced by all, he is convicted by all"* (1 Corinthians 14:24). Paul was concerned to correct a disorderly use of spiritual gifts at Corinth, one that could have been very off-putting to any visitor coming in. He went as far as to say that some visitors might have thought they were mad! By contrast, a healthy church, one which is growing properly, will be a very welcoming environment to visitors. This will be the result of making the best and wisest use of the spiritual gifts given by God. Those visitors will feel welcomed.

It's true that a great deal of the work of evangelism takes place outside of church services. It happens when we meet people where they are. But at some point we would certainly be looking to bring them to hear a presentation of the claims of Christ in a church setting. On that first visit especially, our concern is that they are not disturbed or distracted by anything that's out of order. We've already been thinking about going out and making contacts. In a modern setting we may be known to be active within our community through running a church youth club or by using the church hall for a Parent & Toddler group. As we interact with people on a normal friendly basis, doing useful, practical things for them and with them, there are times when spiritual angles crop up naturally in conversation. Arising out of these chats with contacts, we would be looking to invite someone along to something within a church setting, perhaps after fostering the contact by some more informal means first. At any rate, our desire is that our contacts should not remain mere contacts, but become attenders at suitable church services.

Another concern which was an outstanding obstacle to growth at Corinth was the state of disunity within the church. Paul had this to say to them near the beginning of his letter: *'For it has been declared to me concerning you, my brethren, by those of Chloe's household, that there are contentions among you. Now I say this, that each of you says, 'I am of Paul,' or 'I am of Apollos,' or 'I am of Cephas,' or 'I am of Christ.' Is Christ divided?"* (1 Corinthians 1:11-13) Imagine the reaction of visitors coming in if they could sense this level of disunity. They would hardly be likely to feel the warmth of God's love there, would they? If new or occasional attenders are to progress to become regular attenders, then this is something that will be helped along if they can sense and experience genuine Christian fellowship in the local church setting.

I'm reminded of what Ghandi is reputed to have said when visiting the West. He was asked what he thought of Western civilisation. With his quick legal mind, and even sharper wit, his telling reply was 'I think it would be an excellent idea'. If the question had been posed with more than a dose of the then colonial attitude, Ghandi's response was more than a match for it. In one quick comment he'd clearly implied that he saw nothing any more civilized over there. Yet what if a visitor to a local church was asked: 'what do you think of our Christian fellowship?' and they were to reply, like Ghandi, that they thought it would be a good idea! How tragic if they couldn't see it already functioning - as an obvious reality. Paul had to remind those quarrelsome Corinthians that the cross was the great leveller - every believer stands on that common ground. Paul then went on to talk about God's sovereign choice, and later of the judgement-seat of Christ, then of how all Christians belong to Christ and are represented as forming 'His Body'. Paul also spoke of how the same Spirit is behind all the gifts which believers have, and, most famously perhaps, he spoke to them in chapter thirteen of his first letter about real love, God's love.

Surely the motivation behind the mention of all of these things was to cultivate a greater understanding, a better cooperation and more harmonious relationships between the Christians in the Church at Corinth. These would be things that visitors couldn't help noticing. There is tremendous witness potential if those within the church can authentically model healthy marriages and positive family life - for so many homes are dysfunctional throughout our society. There are thirsty people who are longing to see something that really functions.

When it says in Acts chapter two, of the first Church of God at Jerusalem, that they *'devoted themselves to...the fellowship'* (v.42), that was a very real thing.

Anyone would have been able to see this from surrounding examples of how they cared for each other, and shared the things they had with those among them who were in greater need than themselves. It wasn't a commune, but it was fellowship that really functioned. Fellowship that functions is a real asset in helping to move people from being occasional attenders to becoming regular attenders at church events; not only feeling welcomed, but loved and accepted as well. As well as seeing again the need for a welcoming environment, we've also seen that by cultivating good relationships (and repenting of hindrances whenever necessary), visitors who have first of all felt that they are welcome, will go on to experience real Christian fellowship at first hand - a fellowship that functions! When that happens, contacts become attenders and then become regular attenders with the potential to go further.

11: BUILDING GOD'S BUILDING

The Bible has got so much to say about growing churches that it uses more than one illustration. Not only do we have the picture of plants growing and being cared for in a garden, but each local church is described as a building. The apostle Paul described the church of God at Corinth both as God's cultivated land and as God's building (1 Corinthians 3:9). So that there's no confusion, perhaps we need to remind ourselves that the Bible doesn't use the word 'church' in the modern way of meaning a physical building or place of worship. In Bible times, 'church' meant, quite literally, a gathering of people who were 'called out'. Those who had never heard or responded to the call of God in their lives did not belong in any biblical church.

When Paul described the Church of God at Corinth as God's building, he was meaning the Christian believers who actually formed the church there. He was speaking metaphorically, we might say.

Elsewhere, he gave his view (by the Spirit) of all the churches together forming God's temple. Again, this was not a temple of stone made by human hands. It was Stephen, the first named Christian martyr, who made clear that God doesn't live in buildings like that in this age in which we're called to serve Him (Acts 7:48). God's temple is a spiritual building and, what's more, the picture we're given of it is a dynamic one. Paul spoke of the local New Testament churches of God, viewed overall, as *'growing into a holy temple...a dwelling place of God in the Spirit'* (Ephesians 2:21,22).

So even in this building metaphor, there's still the clear expectation of growth or development. An architect's plan begins to develop from the foundation up. In fact, in another chapter of his letter to the Ephesians, Paul seems to tie together the two images of growth (the one of a garden with plants and the other of a building with foundations) when He prayed *"that [God] would grant [them], according to the riches of His glory, to be strengthened with might through His Spirit in the inner man, that Christ may dwell in [their] hearts through faith; that [they], being rooted and grounded in love, may be able to comprehend with all the saints what is the width and length and depth and height - to know the love of Christ which passes knowledge"* (Ephesians 3:16-19).

Paul's prayer was that they might be 'rooted and grounded'. Notice both ideas together: a garden with plants that are rooted, and a building grounded with a foundation. Just as no tree is stronger than its root system, no building is stronger than its foundation. Good foundations are required to support the rest of the development. Paul had something more to say to the Corinthians about this foundation, and he made the point about it being totally unique when he said: *"According to the grace of God which was given to me, as a wise master builder I have laid the foundation, and another builds on it. But let each one take heed how he builds on it. For no other foundation can anyone lay than that which is laid, which is Jesus Christ. Now if anyone builds on this foundation with gold, silver, precious stones, wood, hay, straw, each one's work will become clear; for the Day will declare it, because it will be revealed by fire; and the fire will test each one's work, of what sort it is. If anyone's work which he has built on it endures, he will receive a reward. If anyone's work is burned, he will suffer loss; but he himself will be saved, yet so as through fire."* (1 Corinthians 3:10-15)

Notice again how the sequence has changed: from "I planted, Apollos watered" to 'I...laid the foundation...another builds on it". Paul was adamant that there could be no other foundation than the one he laid, which was Christ. Paul taught Christ: Christ's teaching. It became known as "the apostles' teaching", because the apostles faithfully delivered what they had received; and, as apostles, they had received it directly from the Lord. The first rule of the building stage is to lay the foundation well. There can be no healthy growth or development if there isn't the correct teaching basis for it all: that's the Lord's own teaching – which today we get from the pen of the apostles in our New Testament.

At the next stage of the building work, as with any works foreman, Paul's concern was with maintaining the build quality. That's where individual responsibility comes in, as we each respond to the foundational teaching of Christ. The biblical churches of God were built on teaching, Christ's teaching. They weren't there because some attractive personality had drawn a following; nor because some tradition offered people a 'feel good factor'. No, Paul just made it totally clear to the Corinthians that their church constitution was as laid down in the apostles' teaching - the same constitution as from the beginning at Jerusalem in Acts chapter two (see v.42).

We say, again, that Christ (His commands) have to be taught with clarity and conviction, in teaching that's cross-centred and Bible-based. When Christ is taught with passion and warmth, and when the teaching is structured and accessible for all, then this rich feeding in the power of the Spirit should have the effect of energizing the church, for the word of Christ is spirit and life. Near the close of our Bible, Jude brings in this matter of our response to the foundational church teaching. He wrote in verse 20 of us building ourselves up in our most holy faith, and linked it to praying in the Spirit and keeping ourselves in the love of God (Jude 20, cf. John 14:15, 21, 23). It's as we keep Christ's commands that we keep ourselves in His love (John

15:10). If we're all enjoying the Word, and the word of Christ is dwelling in our hearts and we're praying Christians (for whom the love of God is a very real thing), then how can it be otherwise than that we'll be built up in our most holy faith? But it won't stop there. If we're richly enjoying God's Word, and if the church is characterized by a learning that lives, then we would hope to see the church built up in numbers.

The Lord graciously adds with reference to the Corner-stone, since all expansion must be in keeping with the foundation that's already laid (Acts 2:5,11 & 1 Peter 2:5,6). It was the apostle Peter who mentioned this in his first letter, and he seemed to have the subject of growth very firmly in mind by chapter two (v.2). He wrote of genuine Christian experience in verse four when he said, 'You have tasted that the Lord is gracious'. It was something real, for the taste left them longing for more. It was to lead onto them continuing to come to Christ - the Christ they knew already as Saviour - for these were growing disciples - and so they were continuing to come to Christ as the cornerstone, continuing to come into obedience to the blueprint of the Lord's foundational teaching for the building of His local churches. And as they continued to do that, Peter speaks of them *"being built up a spiritual house"* (v.5). That really spells out growth and dynamic development, doesn't it - through a learning that lives! Those in the first church at Jerusalem had a learning that lived, for it says, *"They devoted themselves to the apostles' teaching"* (Acts 2:42 NIV). A growing church will have devoted learners, and that means they are those who put it into practice. They don't just admire the teaching; they actually adorn it (Titus 2:10). That's what will attract addition to the church fellowship from among the ranks of those who have already been drawn in to become regular attenders at church services.

Notice that I've haven't said 'populist teaching'. Real growth, healthy growth, doesn't come about by setting out to tell people the things they want to hear. Paul warned Timothy that that kind of message would 'spread like cancer' (2 Timothy 2:17). That's cancerous growth, and Paul warned of those who had *'swerved away from the truth'* (2 Timothy 2:18); and of those who would pander to the *'itching ears'* of their audience (2 Timothy 4:3). Timothy wasn't to be in the numbers game, but rather to present himself approved to God in all that he taught, as someone who *'rightly divided the word of truth'* (2 Timothy 2:15). True church growth can only be brought about by the Spirit working powerfully through the Word of God as it's being taught in clarity and with conviction: and all backed up by abundant evidence in the lives of those in the church that this is a learning that lives!

12: EDIFYING EACH OTHER

A t this stage in our study of growing churches, and what makes them grow, I think it would be good to look at an actual example of a growing church. There's one that we find in Acts chapter nine. Look out for the characteristics of a growing church. *"So the church throughout all Judea and Galilee and Samaria enjoyed peace, being built up; and, going on in the fear of the Lord and in the comfort of the Holy Spirit, it continued to increase" (Acts 9:31 NASB).*

There's nothing random about that list of features that the Holy Spirit has connected with this expanding church. Here was real growth. Its specific recorded characteristics are that: it was being edified; it was going on in the fear of the Lord; it was going on in the comfort of the Holy Spirit; and so it was continuing to increase. I'd like to go through each of these features with you in turn over the course of the remaining chapters in this book. Wouldn't we like to know more of this biblical reality today? Wouldn't we like to see more churches enjoying this kind of growth? They were going forward confidently in the fear of God and in the comfort of the Holy Spirit, and were being edified, that is: were being built up.

Let's begin right there. It says of this church that it was being edified. This is another building word - just as we've already thought about getting the foundational teaching right. We sometimes talk about a building as being an edifice. We've already seen that Paul used the idea of a construction site as one of the pictures he gave of growth. He described the need to build on the right foundation and maintain the build quality. Here we have another description of a growing church, and one which continues the house-building metaphor. What sort of upbuilding ministry is meant here?

The apostle Paul used the same idea in his letter to the church at Ephesus when he wrote to them about the subject of how to promote spiritual growth. If we pay attention to what he says there, we'll get a clearer idea of what makes for growth at the local church level. Notice how he used this same word, 'edifying': *"And He Himself* [the ascended Christ] *gave some to be apostles, some prophets, some evangelists, and some pastors and teachers, for the equipping of the saints for the work of ministry, for the edifying of the body of Christ, till we all come to the unity of the faith and of the knowledge of the Son of God, to a perfect man, to the measure of the stature of the fullness of Christ; that we should no longer be children, tossed to and fro and carried about with every wind of doctrine, by the trickery of men, in the cunning craftiness of deceitful plotting, but, speaking the truth in love, may grow up in all things into Him who is the head - Christ"* (Ephesians 4:11-15).

Paul was certainly writing about growth: the kind of growth that would cause a local church to be seen to be growing. According to Paul how does it comes about? He begins by talking about God-given spiritual gifts. Every believer on the Lord Jesus Christ has at least one spiritual gift from God. We can also check that point out from Peter's words: *"As each one has received a gift, minister it to one another, as good stewards of the manifold grace of God"* (1 Peter 4:10). It's worth emphasizing the point by looking at the same Bible verse but from a different English version: *"Each one should use whatever gift he has received to serve others, faithfully administering God's grace in its various forms"* (1 Peter 4:10 NIV).

Notice that it says 'each one' - each of us is intended to use whatever gift we have in serving others. Christianity is definitely not a spectator sport. It's God's intention that every Christian should become active in ministry, which often means serving God by serving others. Let's go back again to where we started out in Ephesians 4. It was that section about growth that got us started exploring the part played by spiritual gifts. It was speaking about *"equipping...the saints for the work of ministry, for...edifying"*. So there's the sequence: the gifts God gives are to equip us all to serve God and each other with the end result that the local church gets built up and grows.

We'd expect a growing church to be one where those who belong to it (ideally **all** those who belong to it) are active in using their gifts to serve God. In practice, that's going to mean that we each get to know what our main gift is and, in fellowship with others, we work out opportunities for using it to forward God's purposes locally in the lives of others. Spiritually mature believers with whom we serve can help us to identify our gift and ways in which we can put it to use for God's glory and for the upbuilding of the church locally. Hopefully, our own sense of where God is giving the blessing in our lives and service will confirm this.

Perhaps some gifts like those of preaching, teaching, and pastoring are easier to recognize, so maybe it's worth taking a moment to think of how some of the other practical gifts may be identified. Take the gift of 'serving' (Romans 12:7). The word describing this gift suggests a 'waiter'; someone who attends on others. From it, we learn that the work of ministering is a personal service done toward others; one which calls for awareness of the need of others - as we support them through times of difficulty. The work of serving could involve visiting those who are ill, as well as being prepared to do any menial task. It's a behind-the-scenes service.

Good works like those we've mentioned can pave the way for our witnessing when the person on the receiving end is, say, a neighbour who's not yet a Christian. Another gift is simply described as the gift of 'helps' (1 Corinthians 12:28). This appealing little word seems to indicate someone who works alongside others to assist in doing something in which they themselves may not be gifted, but are able to help with. In Luke's Gospel (5:7) there's an example of those in another fishing boat who came to help land the miraculous catch of fish, although they'd not been involved in the work of catching it themselves. Doesn't that point to the fact that in the work of evangelism (which the Lord said was like fishing) there are practical, or maybe technical, roles which assist those who are actually giving out the message? There really is something for everyone to do.

In this book, we've mentioned different stages in the practical growth of a church. Right at the beginning we thought about making contacts in our own local communities. As the work of evangelism progresses, we look (ideally) to see these contacts being brought to church services where they become first of all occasional attenders and then regular attenders. This is prior to them finding their place in the church, having arrived there by means of the biblical steps of salvation, baptism and addition. In practice, we've emphasized that a fellowship that really functions and a learning that really lives are what God has designed to encourage attenders to become regular in their attendance and then become convinced that their place should be in the church.

Another part of the Bible picture of a healthy church concerns a worship that really warms, and when real spiritual worship causes us to present ourselves as surrendered and available for service (Romans 12:1), it's then that we become active in using our spiritual gifts for edification. While many of the gifts will find a direct use inside the church, the scope of others will be felt beyond in the surrounding community. Gifts like serving and being a help can have a real place in evangelism, and so the cycle of growth that has seen an unsaved contact come all the way through to become active in the church can begin all over again, as that person in turn looks to make fresh contacts. And so the gifts build up the church - in every way, including growth in numbers.

Edification, then, is what happens when the whole range of New Testament spiritual gifts are first properly understood, and then put into operation locally, and when everyone feels their responsibility to discover and use their gift from God. It brings about a Christian sense of fulfilment for each churched individual when they discover, develop and discharge their own spiritual giftedness. In New Testament times the range of these gifts found its Biblical expression in churches of God, and led to them growing in spiritual maturity. The overall impression that we're left with is one of collective growth, which is the result of patient labour in local churches operating in line with the gifts contained in them.

13: WALKING FORWARD TOGETHER

In the last chapter, we had our introduction to one of the great Bible verses about a growing church: *"So the church throughout all Judaea and Galilee and Samaria had peace, being edified; and, walking in the fear of the Lord and in the comfort of the Holy Spirit, was multiplied"* (Acts 9:31 American Standard Version). Notice how it speaks of the church 'walking' in the fear of the Lord and in the comfort of the Holy Spirit. It's really that word 'walking' that I'd like us to concentrate on now. Let's try to find out a bit more of what it means.

A different Bible version says: *"So the church throughout all Judea and Galilee and Samaria enjoyed peace, being built up; and, going on in the fear of the Lord and in the comfort of the Holy Spirit, it continued to increase"* (Acts 9:31 NASB). Instead of 'walking', it says 'going on'. That's a fair translation, because behind the word that's translated 'walking' is the idea of something being 'on the move'. This is like an eastern shepherd going out ahead of his sheep (John 10:4). There's a sense of movement and direction and going forward in this word. So one thing's very clear: those Christians in Acts chapter nine were not shrinking back, nor were they simply stagnating. They were going somewhere; they were forward-looking; they were experiencing a dynamic movement that was under the Spirit's direction. It seems reasonable to translate this today into a church with at least some degree of visionary planning, as opposed to one which is determined at all costs to perpetuate the methods and styles of the past. A church like that in Acts 9 would be one which looks to the Bible to define its purposes, and looks to the Lord for guidance as to which methods can be used to best advantage in order to achieve these purposes in the fast-changing times in which we live.

We were thinking in earlier chapters that we've been given the greatest ever mission statement. It was when Jesus said, *"Go therefore and make disciples of all the nations, baptizing them in the name of the Father and of the Son and of the Holy Spirit, teaching them to observe all things that I have commanded you"* (Matthew 28:19-20). That gives a sharp focus on what is our purpose: going forward and making disciples, and seeing these same disciples going forward in baptism and in their understanding of the Lord's teaching. It's all about going forward. It's one thing to see from our Bibles what we should be like and what we should be doing in this whole area of disciple-making, but it's quite another matter getting there.

First of all, we need to take stock of where we are. In taking stock of where we are, we may find a place for conducting a survey in which those who belong to the local church are asked various questions: like what they understand as being the main purposes of their church life; what they would recognize as their own spiritual gift; whether or not they feel they are being equipped to serve; whether they see the opportunities that exist locally for them using their gift...and so on. A practical thing like a survey along these lines can be helpful inasmuch as it helps everyone to become focused on church growth and their own contribution towards it. It's always good to capture fresh suggestions for evangelism, and be alerted to any deficiencies in pastoral care - and anything else that may get flagged up. Not that it has to be done through a survey, of course; that's just one way in which church leaders can take stock. Often a stock-taking exercise like that kind of questionnaire shows up areas of weakness where it appears the local church is falling some way short of its biblical responsibilities.

This process of discovering (or rediscovering) what the Bible requires of us, and where we honestly think we are, can itself give us the motivation to 'narrow the gap'. But what are the main goals of the local church? I think Paul's pastoral letters to Timothy give us a balanced all-round view of its duties. Paul set out standards for a healthy church in the distinct areas of its use of God's Word, its worship, its work for God, its welfare, its witness, and its warfare. Like those about whom we were reading in Acts chapter 9, Paul was forward-looking, as he prepared to hand the baton of ministry over to Timothy.

As we noted earlier, there's a tremendous emphasis on the Word of God throughout the whole of his second letter to him. Timothy was told to 'hold fast the pattern of sound words', to 'rightly divide the word of truth', that he must 'preach the Word', and for the reason that 'all Scripture is given by inspiration of God'. There's no doubt about it: this was to be a learning that lives. 1 Timothy chapter 2 talks about our worshipful approach to God, and about the reverence and orderliness that's required in our public drawing near to God. The public prayers of the local church should always suitably express the 'worth-ship' of God. When they do, that will be prayer that powers the church. Worship is not to be mechanical and dull. Neither is it to be unreflective and flippant; but it is to be from the heart and fervent. A worship that warms occurs when a full attendance brings an ever fresh appreciation of the person and work of the Lord Jesus. In such an appreciation, the Spirit's leading can be detected in an orderly, joyful design. Surely it's true that a growing disciple will be a worshipping disciple; and the church that continually knows a greater sense of God will be a church that's increasing in the most important way of all.

Moving on again to the topic of 'work': there can really be no doubting Paul's message that the local church is to be a place of work for all who are in it – and hard work at that, for Paul compared Christian service to the labour of a hardworking farmer (2:6). Among Paul's favourite words were those used here which stress the strong exertion required in Christian service. We've already seen how the Bible encourages each of us to be active in local church life, using our God-given gift, so that we all may be found to be *useful for the Master* (2:21). If my church isn't growing, I need to ask if I'm a passenger or a worker for God.

Then there was Paul's encouragement to Timothy to witness the good confession: to make confession of his faith in Christ. This is just another reminder that we're all called to be witnesses of the Lord Jesus. The local church is to be like a city set on a hill which cannot be hidden (Matthew 5:14). Witness is certainly another of the purposes of the local church as Paul considered them in his two pastoral letters to Timothy. Regarding welfare, it's interesting to remember that we started out with the example of church-life from Acts chapter 9. This is the same chapter which mentions the death of Dorcas - and does so with reference to *all the widows* (v.39) at Joppa. It's almost as though there's a hint that they somehow formed a recognized group. Paul's pastoral letters give a clear indication of what's meant to be each local church's responsibility for the social welfare of all those belonging to its number, especially the needy. This is the duty of the Christian care that's to be shown to all those who are in real need - first of all to any in the church. Care for all is to be an outstanding feature of church-life, just as it marked out the first ever local church of God at Jerusalem.

This was certainly a growing church and one whose fellowship really functioned. Paul also spoke to Timothy about warfare. Why? Because those in the local church come under attack from the world around. It's a world that makes assaults on a Christian lifestyle. It tempts us with materialism and appeals to us to lower our standards. Adverts bombard us with their enticing messages: the promise of appearing more sophisticated or more admired by others. There's the mentality that says we must keep up with our neighbours. We clutter our lives and lose our cutting-edge. In what can be a very real struggle to draw an acceptable line, it's good to remember that *godliness with contentment is great gain*. More than anything else, perhaps, this is the test: are we content with such things as we have, and are we willing to share? If we're not content, then maybe we're losing the battle.

What we're saying is that a healthy, growing church will be a church that's going on with the Lord, one that's forward-looking in terms of achieving the targets God has set for it. It will be winning the battle against worldiness by encouraging holy living; it will be letting its light shine out clearly; it will be promoting real church fellowship including special care shown to those who need most support; it will be a church known for actively bearing fruit in every good work; where the thrill of worship is a joyful reality; and where sound Bible teaching is its mainstay. Such churches with a vision for going forward will be open to modern approaches that are no less biblical as they reach out to fulfil God's purposes for the local church.

14: CONFIDENTLY GOD-FEARING

Recently, one church survey on growing churches came up with the main conclusion that 'Confident Churches Grow'. It comes back to mind now because there's a link with the topic of this chapter, which has to do with the fear of the Lord. Here's what we find in one of the wise sayings of the book of Proverbs: *"In the fear of the LORD there is strong Confidence"* (Proverbs 14:26). Fear in this sense means 'reverence' rather than 'terror', of course.

The message here is that if we're reverencing God then there's really nothing we need to be afraid of in this life. The sort of confidence that's produced by a sense of the fear of the Lord is definitely one that's got to do with growth. Another thing we discover from our text in Acts chapter nine, is that going forward and continuing in the fear of the Lord was part of the delightful description of that growing church: *"So the church throughout all Judea and Galilee and Samaria enjoyed peace, being built up; and, going on in the fear of the Lord and in the comfort of the Holy Spirit, it continued to increase"* (Acts 9:31 NASB).

A holy boldness, or confidence, was something which characterized the early Christians. We even read of them *"joyfully accepting the plundering of their goods"* (Hebrews 10:34). I don't think we're left in any doubt that this was due to the fact that they had a holy boldness towards God. It characterized their worship (10:19) and the general level of their confident expression of Christian beliefs (3:14). Even under threat, believers in Jerusalem are recorded as praying that *"with all boldness"* they might be granted to speak the word of the Lord (Acts 4:29). Isn't the lesson here that a boldness before God will produce a boldness before men and women? A church which serves in the fear of the Lord will be a church which confidently holds out the word of life. There's no doubt that this was the situation in Acts chapter 9, where we read of this expanding church going forward in the fear of the Lord. What does that mean in practical terms?

Sadly, what the Bible describes as *'the fear of the Lord'* is something we probably don't hear enough about these days. Let's allow the Bible itself to explain: *"The fear of the LORD is to hate evil; pride and arrogance"* (Proverbs 8:13). Of course, that was the attitude of the Lord Jesus in all of His public ministry, and was exactly as Isaiah had predicted of Him: *"His delight is in the fear of the LORD, and He shall not judge by the sight of His eyes, nor decide by the hearing of His ears"* (Isaiah 11:3). The book of Proverbs, with all its wise sayings, has quite a lot to say about the fear of the Lord. This helps us to understand what it is. Those who reject the fear of the Lord are spoken of as hating knowledge and turning away from God's wise counsel to go their own foolish way. Here's how some are described in the very first chapter: *"Because they hated knowledge and did not choose the fear of the LORD, They would have none of my counsel and despised my every rebuke. Therefore they shall eat the fruit of their own way, and be filled to the full with their own fancies"* (Proverbs 1:29-31).

So, basically, I think we can see that the fear of the Lord is associated with avoiding evil. We can do that by allowing ourselves to be guided by God's wise counsel. When we relate this to the local church context, we'd expect to see Christlikeness and the fruit of the Spirit as opposed to attitudes and lifestyles which conform to world trends. There will be a deliberate avoidance of sin based on a shared understanding of the Bible's standards of purity and godliness. Holy living will also be humble living, with the proper level of subjection as the Bible directs - all this in a loving atmosphere where real care is being expressed for each other. We've considered earlier the boldness and growth of the first church of God in Jerusalem. The fear of the Lord was certainly known in it, too. On one occasion which we can read about in Acts, a husband and wife together decided to lie to the Holy Spirit. They were struck down dead by God in summary judgement and, very understandably, we read on that *"great fear came upon all the church and upon all who heard these things...and believers were increasingly added to the Lord, multitudes of both men and women"* (Acts 5:11,14).

It reminds me of another time, in the Old Testament on this occasion, when God's summary judgement fell on a man who had wrongly handled the Ark of the Covenant. When that happened, David - and all who were with him, I'm sure - feared the Lord. We read that: *"David would not remove the ark of the LORD unto him into the city of David: but David carried it aside into the house of Obededom the Gittite. And the ark of the LORD continued in the house of Obededom the Gittite three months: and the LORD blessed Obededom, and all his household"* (2 Samuel 6:10-11 KJV).

Why did David take the ark to the home of Obededom? After all, he was a foreigner. Could it be that this man and his home-life were marked out in that place as demonstrating the fear of the Lord? I think that's how it must have been. The ark of the Lord, the symbol of the Lord's presence, was now in that man's home. What a witness that would have been to the neighbourhood! Did people pop in to see the ark of the testimony which normally was only seen by the high priest of Israel? If Christ is settled down and at home in our hearts through faith (Ephesians 3:17), will our lives not equally express the fear of the Lord and be powerful in their witness among our neighbours? Surely they will. Our home-life is also linked to our church-life, isn't it?

Timothy received instructions from Paul that a man wasn't to be recognized as a church leader unless he had proved himself in the domestic sphere. His home-life had to be beyond reproach. These are standards to which all believers should be aspiring. Peter specifically says of women that their home-life was to be such that unbelieving husbands would be won for the Lord simply by the conduct of their wives - without even a word needing to be spoken (1 Peter 3:1)! The growth we would all most like to see is within our own extended family circles. There are no guarantees that will happen, but the fear of the Lord begins at home, and its witness is telling. One of the famous pictures the Lord gave us of discipleship is a clear picture of growth and how it happens. Jesus said:

"I am the true vine, and My Father is the vinedresser. Every branch in Me that does not bear fruit He takes away; and every branch that bears fruit He prunes, that it may bear more fruit. Abide in Me, and I in you. As the branch cannot bear fruit of itself, unless it abides in the vine, neither can you, unless you abide in Me. I am the vine, you are the branches. He who abides in Me, and I in him, bears much fruit; for without Me you can do nothing. If anyone does not abide in Me, he is cast out as a branch and is withered; and they gather them and throw them into the fire, and they are burned. By this My Father is glorified, that you bear much fruit; so you will be My disciples. If you keep My commandments, you will abide in My love, just as I have kept My Father's commandments and abide in His love." (John 15:1-10)

Growing discipleship involves God's loving discipline. The Lord spoke very plainly about the need for pruning in terms of this picture of growth that He gave. The lesson is for disciples and it's about keeping the Lord's commands - so we can't limit this teaching illustration to our own life in isolation from others. The word 'disciples' is in the plural, and God's commands bring us together with others in service for Him. The God of the vine is also the God of the vineyard (see 1 Corinthians 9:7). Starting with each of us personally, the emphasis for our church-life must be on obedience and intimacy in order for there to be fruitfulness as well as the productiveness that God is looking for. The thought of pruning to increase healthy growth, brings us back full circle to the fear of the Lord in relation to confident church growth.

15: COMFORTING AND BEING COMFORTED

We've been exploring a real example of a growing church. What an inspiring example it is, in Acts 9:31: *"So the church throughout all Judea and Galilee and Samaria enjoyed peace, being built up; and, going on in the fear of the Lord and in the comfort of the Holy Spirit, it continued to increase"* (NASB). Already we've thought about God's plan for the building up, or edifying, of local churches - and seen how He means us to make full use of the spiritual gifts He has given us for that edification to happen. The powerful working of spiritual gifts in daily operation should give a real sense of the presence of God. That's the thought that we move on to now as we consider the next fact presented here - that this growing church, this church that was moving forward, was doing so in the comfort of the Holy Spirit, as well as in the fear of the Lord.

What does it mean to go forward in the comfort of the Holy Spirit? The same word 'comfort' is used repeatedly by Paul near the beginning of his first letter to the Church of God at Corinth. So let's turn our attention to that little section, and look out for the words 'comfort' and 'consolation'. They are really the same thing. Let's see if we can catch a sense of the reality of God's working in the lives of those Christians at Corinth. It seems as if the presence of God among them was relieving their hurts as well as touching the lives of others through them.

"Blessed be the God...of all comfort, who comforts us in all our tribulation, that we may be able to comfort those who are in any trouble, with the comfort with which we ourselves are comforted by God. For as the sufferings of Christ abound in us, so our consolation also abounds through Christ. Now if we are afflicted, it is for your consolation and salvation, which is effective for enduring the same sufferings which we also suffer. Or if we are comforted, it is for your consolation and salvation. And our hope for you is steadfast, because we know that as you are partakers of the sufferings, so also you will partake of the consolation." (2 Corinthians 1:3-7)

This was a church where the nearness of God was felt in all the troubles that they were experiencing. It was a local church where the presence of God was being felt in a very real way. The word 'comfort' actually contains the idea of God drawing near; of Him being called to their side, for their assistance. The Bible in the Old Testament records so many times of Joseph that the Lord was with him (e.g. Genesis 39). He was someone who knew more than his fair share of troubles, but in and through them all, God's presence was with him and ensured him success and a growing influence.

The troubles of the Corinthians had also brought God close to them and made Him very real to them. They were enjoying the relief and encouragement that His presence had brought. Having really sensed that themselves, they were now in a position to serve wider needs in their locality. When they came across neighbours or friends who were struggling, they now found that they could dispense comfort to them. This was from their own experience of knowing comfort when they had been in difficulty. So they were engaging the needs of the surrounding community in relevant ways. It's in our weakness that we are made strong; trouble in our lives causes us to draw near to God, and when we do that He promises to draw near to us. But that's not the only way of experiencing God's power and presence with us.

Another way that God draws alongside us is through His Word as well as by means of the Holy Spirit's gifts. Paul used the word 'comfort' in this way too, when he said to his friends at Rome that: *"whatever things were written before were written for our learning, that we through the patience and comfort of the Scriptures might have hope"* (Romans 15:4). These things are usually linked in our experience, are they not? When in trouble or needing help, we reach for our Bibles, and God, through the ministry of His Word, draws near for our help or maybe as the gift of another believer is used to share a spiritual message with us. How important it is that we show the reality of our faith and of our walk with the Lord, by sharing the good things of His Word with each other. These are things that can really encourage and uplift. The word 'comfort' is used in this way too, when Paul says, again to his Christian friends at Rome:

"Having then gifts differing according to the grace that is given to us, let us use them: if prophecy, let us prophesy in proportion to our faith; or ministry, let us use it in our ministering; he who teaches, in teaching; he who exhorts, in exhortation; he who gives, with liberality; he who leads, with diligence; he who shows mercy, with cheerfulness." (Romans 12:6-8)

In a previous chapter we were thinking about the gifts as bringing edification; well, part of that is when they bring us encouragement. And Paul talks of specific gifts here: the gifts of prophesying, serving, teaching, exhorting, giving, leading and showing mercy. In that list, the gift described as 'exhorting' or 'comforting' is the gift of encouragement. I'm sure we've all known times when someone has said just the right thing to us at exactly the right time, and we found it to be a real encouragement from the Lord. This gift of encouragement has been translated as the gift of stimulating the faith of others. Remember, it's still the word 'comfort', and we began by thinking of a church that was growing because it was moving forward in the comfort of the Holy Spirit. We'd expect a church like that to be a church where faith was being stimulated. It seems to me that, through this gift of exhortation, the Holy Spirit uncovers and resolves problems that, if left, would prevent spiritual growth taking place among Christians.

Another way of looking at this same gift of encouragement is to see it working through Christians as they stimulate each other towards discharging their duties – encouraging each other, too, towards commitment, and greater productivity. Many things can hold us back even as Christians. For some it may be an inability to overcome feelings of bitterness or resentment; for others it may be frustration that inclines to mild depression; or losing the battle with impure thoughts. Trying to change the way people behave isn't usually effective until they can be helped to change the way they think. That's where this practical spiritual gift of encouragement comes in. In a friendly and helpful way, the encourager begins to explore with the person concerned what their difficulty seems to be. As the conversation develops, the encourager, in a caring way, tunes into the person's negative feelings. Are they coming across as angry, afraid or feeling guilty?

It may be that we've noticed that a Christian at church doesn't get involved with anything. As we show interest and make ourselves available for an encouraging chat, we gradually pick up on the fact that they are not taking part in projects because they desperately want to steer clear of any responsibility - and that this is due to a fear of failure on their part. In helping them to see that this, really, is unbiblical behaviour, the encourager may begin to uncover long-standing opinions that the person holds of himself or herself. Perhaps from earliest years they have been told 'You're no good', 'You can't do that', 'Let me do it for you'. And so they have come to believe it and to behave accordingly.

An encourager can do no better than to emphasize that what we can do as Christians is only in the strength the Lord provides (Philippians 4:13). Depending on ourselves is misplaced in Christian service. We are to be as branches in the vine which is Christ (John 15), and to draw all our resources from Him in exactly the same way as a branch depends on the vine that it's growing on. If we can encourage someone to discover that they really do have a particular gift from God and to depend on Him in faith for how to use it, then we've helped to uncover and resolve something that was an obstacle to growth, and we've done it by the Spirit's help through using the gift of encouragement. The best way to encourage someone like that is by following the good advice of the Bible itself. James tells us to be good listeners: *"Be swift to hear, slow to speak"* (James 1:19), he says. An example is held up for us in Ezekiel. The Bible says that, when he was delivering his message, *"he sat where they sat"* (Ezekiel 3:15).

It's true, isn't it, that people need to know how much we care before they care how much we know. They need to know that we're on their side, and we need to show that we can also see the thing from their point of view. God's own dealings with Jonah (Jonah 4:4) teach us the value of asking sensitive, but not intrusive, questions; while Paul, in writing to the Ephesians, (Ephesians 4:15) reminds us to speak the truth only in love; if it's loving then it can be received. May we know what it is to go forward in the encouragement that the Holy Spirit provides through His gifts, and with a real sense of the reality of God's presence in our church-life.

16: INCREASING INCREMENTALLY

As we conclude our study of church growth, we return one final time to our text from Acts 9: *"So the church throughout all Judea and Galilee and Samaria enjoyed peace, being built up; and, going on in the fear of the Lord and in the comfort of the Holy Spirit, it continued to increase"* (NASB). At this point, we're concerned with the very last thing said of it: that it continued to increase. In Jerusalem itself, in those early days of Christianity, the number of Christians grew and grew. We read of a hundred and twenty (Acts 1:15), then three thousand more (2:41,42), and then there's mention of at least five thousand (4:4), and then 'myriads' or 'multitudes' (5:14) - as if they'd lost count of how many were added to them!

But this wasn't like some modern concepts of a 'mega-church', boasting congregations of many thousands. The believers at Jerusalem were subdivided into various companies. We read of disciples going to their own company (Acts 4:23 KJV). This would soon have become a practical necessity, what with the difficulties of finding suitable accommodation and hostile authorities harassing them, among other things. Growth materialized in those smaller companies belonging to the Jerusalem church. So there's nothing new in principle about the contemporary experience that subdividing a larger unit into multiple cell-groups makes the prospect of growth more realistic. It allows for fuller participation and development of spiritual gifts, and broader scope for the training of disciples. Christianity has not been designed as a spectator sport, so it can only follow that sharing out the opportunities and responsibilities is as beneficial as it is biblical. Perhaps it's an encouragement to smaller churches to see from the Bible that smallness isn't necessarily an impediment to growth - but rather the opposite.

In everything we say about the experience of the expanding church at Jerusalem, we have to keep in mind the absolutely basic principle that it is God who gives the increase (1 Corinthians 3:7). Real biblical growth isn't achieved by simply adopting smart business techniques, novel methods or giving people more of what they want. God brings about growth from things as small as a grain of mustard seed. It's quite remarkable that the word 'church' is used in the singular in our Acts chapter nine text. It really faces us up with the reality of how unified these early Christians were. We know that by this time there were, in fact, many churches throughout Judea (Galatians 1:22), not to mention Galilee and Samaria - and yet they are spoken of as one. So at Jerusalem there were many companies forming one church in that city. Across the named provinces, there were many other churches answering to that first one in Jerusalem, but such was the unity of their fellowship together, they could all be bracketed together in the singular here.

Smallness isn't necessarily an impediment to growth, but it all has to come right down to each of us as individuals in the final analysis. The Lord started Christianity off with a small hand-picked group of followers. Even among themselves, at the very beginning, Andrew reached out to his brother Simon Peter. The secret of effective spiritual multiplication or reproduction lies in the 'one-reach-one' strategy or what we might style as 'the Andrew principle'. It's something we do and pray about within the support framework of the local church and the encouragement it gives to us. I wonder if three words from the old Bible language can help us. They are easy Greek words: 'pathos', 'ethos' and 'logos'. They are recognizable as the words from which we've got our modern words of sympathy, ethics and logical. They also share with us three practical secrets of increasing church growth. Pathos, as well as giving us the word 'sympathy', also gave us the word 'passion'. We're thinking of passion in the sense of love; our love for those without the knowledge of Christ as their personal Saviour. The poetess Amy Carmichael penned the words: 'Oh for a passionate passion for souls, oh for a love that burns!'

The searching question for us all is: does that reflect our own heart's yearning for our unsaved friends, neighbours and colleagues? The apostle Paul was a tremendous example of this pathos or passion, this love for the lost. Let's read about his heart of love from the second chapter of the first letter he wrote to the local Church at Thessalonica: *"So, affectionately longing for you, we were well pleased to impart to you not only the gospel of God, but also our own lives, because you had become dear to us"* (1 Thessalonians 2:8).

His love for these former pagans is really captured there. He described it as 'affectionate longing'. From before they were saved through to the time of his later nurturing their immature Christian lives; he loved them with God's own love for them, and he expressed it in his open lifestyle towards those who were dear to him. Love is the greatest apologetic. There's a persuasiveness in speech and actions if they are loving. As we said earlier, people don't care how much we know until they know how much we care. In all these ways we need to be sensitive to everyone who is a seeker and to present ourselves in such a way as a local church that our services are welcoming and accessible to these seekers.

We mentioned Paul a moment ago to illustrate his passion and his love for the lost. From the same place we read from earlier, Paul went on to say: *"For you remember, brethren, our labor and toil; for laboring night and day, that we might not be a burden to any of you, we preached to you the gospel of God. You are witnesses, and God also, how devoutly and justly and blamelessly we behaved ourselves among you who believe"* (1 Thessalonians 2:9-10). There's no doubt that Paul worked hard to practice what he preached. He and his companions behaved themselves "devoutly and justly and blamelessly". You could say their conduct was totally ethical. This is where the second of those three Greek words comes in: the word 'ethos'. It's all about integrity: having our life consistent with our lip. I believe it was Francis of Asissi who said that in witnessing for the Lord we should 'if necessary use words'. That's not to say we're not to be ready to speak - Peter says we that are to be (1 Peter 3:15) - but earlier in the same chapter (1 Peter 3:1) he encouraged wives with unbelieving husbands to attempt to live before them day to day in such a way that they might win them 'without the word'. In the intimate scrutiny of the home-life that was real integrity they were being called to model!

Paul the apostle never seemed to be at a loss for words whenever there was an appropriate opportunity to back up his lifestyle evangelism. He could say, again to his Thessalonian friends: *"We have been approved by God to be entrusted with the gospel, even so we speak, not as pleasing men, but God who tests our hearts"* (1 Thessalonians 2:4). There was no flattery with Paul. His was uncompromising teaching. Paul reasoned and persuaded with words of the Spirit's wisdom (Acts 18:4; 1 Corinthians 2). That's where our third and last Greek word fits in: the word 'logos'. The Christian faith is neither blind nor illogical; it's a reasonable faith. In an age of scientific naturalism, of intellectual and moral relativism and of theological pluralism, it will help us to know what people around us believe, and to understand why it is that they believe it. We need to anticipate what points of contact there are, and how we can build from there in communicating God's truth to them from the standpoint of the Bible, the Word of God.

With 'pathos', 'ethos' and 'logos', our communication can still be effective! It's important that we understand (and even use) the culture we live in, as we penetrate it to fulfil the Lord's great commission of

'Go into all the world'. In the days of the Old Testament – with God's people in the Promised Land - their holiness was partly defined by their disengagement from other peoples. In no way has God's standard of holiness for His people today been lowered, but our God-given policy or mandate is to penetrate our culture – to go into the world - and not to be disengaged from it. Again Paul the evangelist made this point forcibly to the Church of God at Corinth: *"I wrote to you in my epistle not to keep company with sexually immoral people. Yet I certainly did not mean with the sexually immoral people of this world, or with the covetous, or extortioners, or idolaters, since then you would need to go out of the world"* (1 Corinthians 5:9-10).

Our difference is to be visible in the silent witness of lives of integrity; but we're to identify with those around us out of a deep loving concern for them. If we can so commend Christianity, by God's almighty help, then surely we'll see churches growing - and that increase will be sometimes thirtyfold, sometimes sixtyfold, and sometimes one hundredfold!

FURTHER TITLES IN THIS SERIES

If you've enjoyed reading this book, first of all please consider taking a moment to leave a positive review on Amazon! Secondly, you my be interested to know that, at the date of the publishing of this book, the Search For Truth library now stands at over 40 titles; each contains excellent reading material in a down-to-earth and conversational style, covering a wide range of topics from Bible character studies, theme studies, book studies, apologetics, prophecy, Christian living and more. The simplest way to access this material for purchase is by visiting Brian's Amazon author page:

- Amazon.com: http://amzn.to/1u7rzIA
- Amazon.co.uk: http://amzn.to/YZt5zC

Alternatively, the books can also be found simply by searching for the specific title or "Search For Truth Series" on Amazon. Paperback versions can also be purchased from Hayes Press at www.hayespress.org.

A flavour of some of the books in the library are below:

A Legacy of Kings…Israel's Chequered History

Apart from the most famous kings, such as David and Solomon, many of the rest of the kings of the Old Testament have faded into obscurity - the life-lessons that can be applied to the lives of Christians are often over-looked as a result. This book rectifies this by bringing twelve of these kings back into the spotlight. You'll encounter good kings, bad kings, good kings that went bad and bad kings that came good! All of them, though, have something important to teach and challenge us as we look to serve the great and faultless King Himself - Jesus Christ. If Jotham, Rehoboam, Hezekiah, Manasseh and the rest have become strangers to you - why not get reacquainted?

Tomorrow's Headlines – Bible Prophecy

This book provides some key principles for unlocking the meaning of Bible prophecy and surveys what the Bible says about the future, primarily from the books of Daniel and Revelation. Topics and questions include:
- Will there ever be a United States of Europe?
- Will there be a single world currency?
- What is the critical position of Israel in God's purposes?
- Will the temple be rebuilt in Jerusalem?
- What can we know about the Antichrist?
- Will Jesus Christ return once, or twice?
- What is the role of Babylon in the end times?
- What is the significance of the spread of Islam?

Overcoming Objections to Christian Faith

This book provides a concise introduction to answering 10 key objections to the Christian faith by giving a number of insightful illustrations and Biblical references which all Christians can use to help them give "a reason for the hope that is within us"and whet the appetite for further research on each question in greater depth:

• Why do the innocent suffer?

- Don't all religions lead to God?
- What about the heathen?
- Isn't the Christian experience only psychological?
- Are the miracles possible?
- Isn't the Bible full of errors?
- Won't a good life get me to heaven?
- How can you believe in hell and a God of love?
- Hasn't science done away with the need for faith?
- What about all the bloodshed in the name of religion?

Life, the Universe...and Ultimate Answers

This book grapples with some of the big questions of life from a Christian perspective, with the following chapter headings:

1. Can We Really Experience God?
2. Is Life Accidental Or Purposeful?
3. Does Life Have Real Value?
4. What's The Meaning of Life?
5. A Personal Hope
6. Is There Any Evidence for God?
7. Is There Evidence For Jesus And The Resurrection?
8. Reasons To Believe: Creation
9. Reasons To Believe: Conscience
10. Reasons To Believe: Communication
11. Reasons To Believe: Christ

Power Outage: Christianity Unplugged

This book pinpoints 11 key ways in which a Christian can experience a lack of God's power in their discipleship experience. The first six chapters deal with actions and character traits that quench the Holy Spirit, and the final five chapters focuses on different ways that we can misuse God's Word, with the same effect - loss of power. As usual, Brian brings a number of Bible illustrations to make his point as well as reflecting on the experience of a number of well-known Christians, including the Wesley brothers.

1. Don't Pray
2. Compromise Your Separation to God
3. Let Sin Enter Your Life

4. Be Proud
5. Be Self-indulgent
6. Be Greedy
7. Invalidate God's Word
8. Neglect God's Word
9. Peddle God's Word
10. Adulterate God's Word
11. Wrongly Divide God's Word

Edge of Eternity - Approaching the End of Life

This book was written by at the request of many people who have found it very difficult to witness to someone who was nearing the end of their lives, either through terminal illness or old age. How could they find a way to tactfully and gently raise the matter of eternal future at this difficult and stressful time?

Brian provides a helpful way to do this by drawing from parts of Luke's gospel which are all connected to death or near-death experience in some way. The gospel is clearly presented in a gentle way with the intention of winning someone to Jesus Christ even at the very end. This book, however, is also a very useful witnessing tool to anyone who has not yet become a Christian.

Double Vision – The Insights of Isaiah

The Old Testament book of Isaiah can be difficult to understand. This book provides the key to open up Isaiah's message by explaining the "double vision" model that God used in speaking through the prophet. While what much of what Isaiah said had a current application to the people he was speaking to, there was usually a double meaning which either spoke of the coming of Jesus Christ hundreds of years later, or of events which are still yet in our future. This book is bound to leave you more aware of, and appreciating more fully, the sovereignty of God and his gracious dealings with both Israel and followers of Jesus Christ.

Praying With Paul

Prayer is one of the greatest assets that a Christian could possess, but sometimes it seems to be a real challenge to make it a full part of our devotional life. Brian examines the way the great prayer warrior himself - the apostle Paul - approached prayer. What were the key things that Paul prayed about and how did he do it? Paul was an expert in how to have a productive prayer life with real intimacy with God. There's no better example of the practice of prayer that we can follow - may it challenge us all to a more productive prayer life in the secret place! A bonus book, Passing the Baton, also features in this book, and takes a look at 4 important relationships in the Bible and the handover of service for God from one to the other.

Unlocking Hebrews

The letter to the Hebrews has been called "the forgotten letter of the New Testament". But, as Brian outlines in this little book, the letter contains a marvellous, divine revelation that is not found anywhere else in the Bible! The writer of the letter is concerned that new believers might be soon be walking away from their new-found faith and reverting back to Judaism. He passionately explains through a series of "warnings" exactly what they will be missing, the unique superiority of Jesus Christ, but also an amazing insight into the location of the collective worship of God, which remains unchanged 2,000 years later!

They Met At The Cross – Five Encounters With Jesus

Brian discusses what happened when five very different people met Jesus at the cross:
Chapter 1: Pontius Pilate – Under Pressure
Chapter 2: Simon Of Cyrene - Under Obligation
Chapter 3: Barabbas - Under Conviction
Chapter 4: Joseph Of Arimathea - Under Cover
Chapter 5: The Centurion – Under Authority

Other Titles

- An Unchanging God?
- The Kingdom of God – Past, Present or Future?
- God's Appointment Calendar: The Feasts of Jehovah
- Seeds – A Potted Bible History
- AWOL! Bible Deserters and Defectors
- The Way – New Testament Discipleship
- 5 Sacred Solos – The Truths That The Reformation Recovered
- Salt & The Sacrifice of Christ
- Turning The World Upside Down – Seven Revolutionary Ideas That Changed The World
- Windows To Faith
- The Visions of Zechariah
- The Last Words of Jesus
- James – Epistle of Straw
- Closer Than A Brother – Christian Friendship
- Experiencing God in Ephesians
- About The Bush – The Life of Moses
- Trees of the Bible
- Once Saved, Always Saved?
- Abraham: Friend of God
- After God's Own Heart: The Life of David
- Knowing God: Reflections on Psalm 23
- Jesus: What Does The Bible Really Say?
- No Compromise!
- The Glory of God
- Jesus: Son Over God's House
- The Way: New Testament Discipleship
- The Tabernacle: God's House of Shadows
- Esther: A Date With Destiny

SEARCH FOR TRUTH RADIO BROADCASTS

Search for Truth Radio has been a ministry of the Churches of God (see www.churchesofgod.info) since 1978. Free Search for Truth podcasts can be listened to online or downloaded at four locations:

- At SFT's own dedicated podcast site:
  www.searchfortruth.podbean.com
- Via Itunes using the podcast app (search for Search For Truth)
- On the Churches of God website:
  (http://www.churchesofgod.info/search_for_truth_radio_progra mmes.php)
- On the Transworld Radio website:
  (http://www.twr360.org/programs/ministry_id,103)

If you have enjoyed reading one of our books or listening to a radio broadcast, we would love to know about that, or answer any questions that you might have. Contact us at:

- Church of God, Leicester, LE5 6LN England
- P.O. Box 748, Ringwood, Victoria 3134, Australia
- P.O.Box 70115, Chilomoni, Blantyre, Malawi
- Web site: www.searchfortruth.org.uk
- Email: sft@churchesofgod.info

ABOUT THE AUTHOR

Responding to God's call in his life Brian Johnston left his post as a UK government scientist in 1987 to become a fulltime Bible teacher and evangelist on behalf of the Churches of God (**www.churchesofgod.info**). For many years, he has been spending much of his time in missionary church-planting activity in Belgium and the Philippines. He also anchors Search for Truth Radio and is an editor of Needed Truth magazine (see **www.neededtruth.info**). He has authored the book Exploring Issues of Life. He is married to Rosemary, and they have two children, Michael and Anna.

Made in the USA
Columbia, SC
13 January 2019